ENDURING
HARDSHIPS

Survival by Faith and Works in Our
Uncharted Territories

Run with
perseverance
the race
marked out
for you.
Heb 12:1

Ruw and I
wishing you
abundant joy
and blessings
in reading
my book.

Joseph Chimbanda

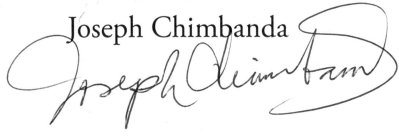

ISBN 978-1-63844-017-8 (paperback)
ISBN 978-1-63903-587-8 (hardcover)
ISBN 978-1-63844-018-5 (digital)

Christian Faith Publishing, Inc.
832 Park Avenue
Meadville, PA 16335
www.christianfaithpublishing.com

Printed in the United States of America

Angola, Africa

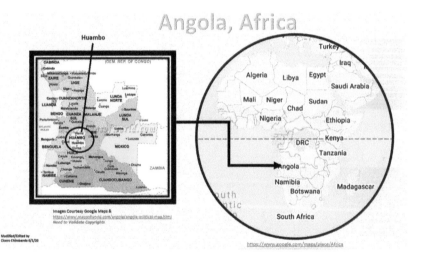

Huambo

(DEM. REP. OF CONGO)

Contents

Foreword

I am honored that Joe and Ana asked me to write this. I know them well, respect them greatly, and admire their Christianity and love of all people. Helping edit their book became a labor of love. I could hardly wait to see what would unfold on the next page. Their biblical and other quotes are amazingly relevant for every aspect of their lives. I concluded that their inspirational story needs to be read by as many as possible.

Joe is both older and younger than me. (Read this book to see why and how.) He has been a good friend for over forty years. I knew him as Jose Chimbanda until he celebrated US citizenship by legally changing his name to Joseph John Chimbanda. (His parents had changed their names when they became Christians.)

Joseph and Ana have been diplomats for Christianity and their race. They have experienced racial discrimination but handled it self-lessly without stopping their love for those involved. I believe anyone having a serious disagreement with either of them could look in a mirror to see the one at fault.

Joseph and Ana were both fortunate to have found one another, fallen in love, and gotten married. They made an extremely strong team nurturing and rearing strong, productive, and caring children. Even with their family strength, I believe that they truly put God first, family second, and others a close third.

I saw Ana break down in tears when remembering the bodies and body parts stacked in a building as she looked for relatives and friends during the Angolan civil war. She faced many difficulties and much danger with her young family after Joe came to school in the

United States. She resorted to some trickery to escape into Portugal where they were stranded, unable to legally leave. Eventually, an immigration loophole enabled them to join Joe in the United States.

Throughout their lives, many hardships, barriers, and challenges tested their physical, mental, and spiritual strength. They agree that their faith in God enabled them to survive, endure, and eventually thrive.

In the United States, they adapted and succeeded. Joe's distance running became phenomenal; as did Ana's service as a nurse. I am among many who feel very blessed by having known Joseph and Ana Chimbanda. I am prayerfully hopeful that their many friends and other readers will be inspired to recommend this book to others and make generous donations to the Chimbanda Scholarship Fund under the umbrella of the Advancing the Gospel in Angola, Inc. (AGA), a 501c3 nonprofit organization, to benefit Angolan children. All donations will be tax deductible.

—Harold Brown, Christian brother,
friend, and first-time editor

Preface

I wrote this book to tell of our struggles and survival by faith and to inspire others to serve God and His people. For over forty years my wife, Ana and I have been sharing our experiences with many people who always encouraged us to write our story of struggles, danger, survival, persistence, faith, hope, and love.

We are not ashamed that we are descended from peasants in Angola, Africa. They were ordinary people whose extraordinary work was caring for their families despite major challenges, limited resources, and few alternatives. Our parents were hardworking farmers with a few acres. Fortunately, they were faithful to the Lord and believed in the importance of education and family. Their sacrificial love was amazingly important to us.

> I wrote this book to tell of our struggles and survival by faith and to inspire others to serve God and His people. For over forty years my wife, Ana and I have been sharing our experiences with many people who always encouraged us to write our story of struggles, danger survival, persistence, faith, and love.

Yes, our parents and God were partners in caring for us. God, Who worked in our past, is working in our present and will work as we age into the future.

It is miraculous that He would work with us from before we were born and during our earthly days until He calls us to heaven where we are going to rejoice forever. We ask God for His ineffable help as we record the highlights of our lives. Our experiences of childhood, hardships, challenges, hard work, endurance, and success should be recorded for our descendants and others.

> It is miraculous that He would work with us from before we were born and during our earthly days until He calls us to heaven where we are going to rejoice forever.
>
> Never...forget what you have seen the Lord do for you. Do not let these things escape from your mind as long as you live! And be sure to pass them on to your children and grandchildren... That way, they will learn to fear me as long as they live, and they will be able to teach my laws to their children. (Deuteronomy 4:9–10 NLT)

We want to inspire people in their times of special need. Pandemics are killing people, separating families, and paralyzing people's lives. Injustice, violence, and racial unrest are huge issues. Throughout the world, unstable economics, natural disasters, wars, and terrorism are major problems. As Christians, we should be ready and willing to carry His ministry. We need to be peacemakers, forgivers, and reconcilers. We need to be prepared by reading and obeying the Bible so that it is ingrained in our hearts. The apostle Paul exhorts us to be letters:

> You show that you are a letter from Christ, the result of our ministry, written not with ink but with the Spirit of the living God, not on tablets of stone but on tablets of human hearts. (2 Corinthians 3:3 NIV)

However, troubles will always exist. Even Jesus warned His disciples,

> In this world you will have trouble. But take heart, I have overcome the world. (John 16:33 NIV)

Moreover, one of the authors of Psalm said,

> We will not hide them (things) from their children; we will tell the next generation the praiseworthy deeds of the Lord, His power, and the wonders He has done; so the next generation would know them, even the children yet to be born, and they in turn would tell their children. Then they would put their trust in God and would not forget His deeds but would keep His commands. (Psalm 78:4 and 6–7 NIV)

There are biblical stories that also influenced us to write. Stephen's speech to the Sanhedrin was about telling the story of ancestors in Acts 7. Paul told his story of conversion in Acts 22:1–21. I read the book *Sword and Scalpel* by Dr. Robert Foster, the Angolan and former Zambian missionary. I was inspired by his character, integrity, and love for Africans. His book made me want to share our experiences and inspiration.

I write our story to thank and honor God for His provision, protection, and guidance, and as tributes to our parents and others who came into our lives with their acts of kindness. Successful people need the help of family, friends, and others. We are truly thankful to have had the needed encouragement and support. I am definitely not writing for money but for more people to realize that blessings are available.

Introduction to Our Story

> "Before I formed you in the womb I knew you, and before you were born I consecrated you; I have appointed you a prophet to the nations." Then I said, "Alas, Lord God!"... But the Lord said to me, do not say, "I am a youth," because everywhere I send you, you shall go, and all that I command you, you shall speak. (Jeremiah 1:5–7 NASB)

Ana Isabel is my best friend, wife, soul mate, and strength of over fifty years and mother of our five children. She was also a strong contributor to our family's survival and to this writing endeavor. We were born and grew up in separate mission stations but met as late teenagers in the city of Nova Lisboa (now Huambo) in Angola, Africa. Now, in 2020, we are in our seventies and living comfortably. However, we remember well the circumstances, hardships, challenges, and danger that put our livelihoods, family unity, and even our lives at risk. Any of several "close calls" could have prevented our descendants from ever existing, much less thriving as they have. We believe it is important that information of our childhoods, challenges, failures, endurance, family, and faith be known to our descendants and others. We hope to encourage readers to appreciate their own circumstances and serve God and His people.

We were born to poor hardworking loving Christian parents in beautiful Angola, Africa, in the 1940s. Despite major health risks and challenges, we survived, learned, fell in love, married, and worked hard building our life together. Soon after we had achieved comfortable living conditions, I left for college in the United States. Very soon my wife and our five young children faced terrible danger due to the collapse of the government and the resulting civil war. Our safe and peaceful lives and material possessions were quickly gone. Ana, alone, had to protect and nurture our children under very risky circumstances for almost four years of fear, frustration, worry, and prayer.

At Ball State University in Muncie, Indiana, I went through eight horrendous months of not knowing whether my family was alive in a war-torn Angola. Then when my family was relatively safe but living illegally in Portugal, we had nineteen months of battling poverty, legalities, and bureaucracies before we could reunite in the United States. We credit God and His people for protection, care, help, and guidance that empowered our successes. Prayers were and are powerful!

Hard work, help from God, friends, and a little trickery ultimately permitted us to reunite in the United States. Much motivation and effort to learn, adapt, improve, and succeed plus sacrifices and faith enabled us to survive and later thrive with a new environment, language, and culture.

Each and every day is a new normal, a chance for new beginnings, new people, places, opportunities, and poignant moments. Of course, sorrows, disappointments, mishaps, inconveniencies, and struggles are often among the circumstances. Finally, unexpected, uncomfortable, and undesirable changes are always possible as uncharted territory is explored. All of the above were among the experiences detailed in this book. Enduring hardships describes our story well.

As I write, some parts make me laugh, and others bring me to tears. As Adam Hamilton in his book *Why?* wrote,

> Because we are human, our story is bound to include sin and adversity, conflict and fear, despair and death. But apart from turning to God, our stories will miss out on the correspond-

ing elements of forgiveness, victory, reconciliation, peace, hope, redemption and love… When we write we invite God to collaborate with us, our story becomes one of redemption and love and hope.

Currently in 2020, we feel we have been blessed in innumerable ways to the extent that we can try to help others. We believe we have justification and almost an obligation to share our life story.

(Because our backgrounds were very similar, Ana's biography won't be written in detail. Basically, whenever I refer to my parents, I intend to honor her parents for equal accomplishments under similar difficulties.)

The Geography of Angola

(See map inside front cover)

Our native country, Angola, is situated in west-central Africa and is roughly square in shape. It is the largest country in sub-Saharan Africa. It is twice the size of Texas. As of 2020, its population is almost thirty-three million. Angola is boarded by the Democratic Republic of Congo (formerly Zaire) to the north and east, Namibia to the south, and Zambia to the east. To the west lies the Atlantic Ocean. Along the coast is a lowland area, which, at its widest point, extends about a hundred miles (160 kilometers) inland. From the eastern side of this plain, the land gradually rises toward the large plateau. Angola is divided into eighteen provinces. The northern region of the country has the three provinces of Cabinda, Zaire, and Uige. To the south is a region centered on Luanda province. To the east and south of Luanda province, there are four provinces: Kuanza North, Malange, Bengo, and Kuanza Sul. The richest agricultural land is found in the central highlands region that includes the provinces of Huambo, Bie, and Huila. The two coastal provinces in the southwest, Benguela and Namibe, have a dryer climate. The inland provinces of Cunene and Kuando Kubango have an arid climate. Finally, there are the eastern inland provinces of Moxico, Lunda North, and Lunda South. Angola's capital is the city of Luanda.

The History of Angola

Early Angola was inhabited by hunters and gatherers, known as Bushmen, Khosian, or San with an elementary knowledge of iron making. There was a migration of Bantu-speaking people from what was known as Cameroon in early AD 500. Then there was a later migration of Bantu speakers from eastern Africa. By the beginning of the sixteenth century, nearly all of Angola was populated by Bantu speakers. As farming developed, some family groups achieved positions of power based on ownership of cattle. There was a creation of kingdoms, the large one the kingdom of Kongo. To the south, there was the smaller Ndongo kingdom. To the east was the Lunda kingdom, which benefited from the planting of new crops (corn and cassava) from America acquired indirectly from the Portuguese. In 1483, a Portuguese explorer named Diogo Cao arrived in the region which he called "Angola," derived from an African word for *king*, *ngola*.

Angolan Freedom Fighters (1952–1975) and Civil War (1975–2002)

In 1952, five hundred Angolan Africans petitioned the United Nations to force Portugal to grant independence to Angola. Nationalist organizations soon began agitating for the end of foreign rule. The Popular Movement for the Liberation of Angola (MPLA) was formed in 1956 and led by Agostinho Neto, a doctor and popular poet who adopted a communist ideology and gained support from the Soviet Union. The National Front for the Liberation of Angola (FNLA) led by Holden Roberto had support from the United States. In 1966, Jonas Savimbi broke off from FNLA to form the National Union for the Total Independence of Angola (UNITA) supported by the United States.

By 1974, Portugal had lost about nine thousand soldiers in Angola. Military leaders were tired of fighting a war they could not win and were frustrated with their government. On April 25, 1974, Portuguese general Spinola led a successful military coup against Marcello Caetano, the successor of Salazar who died in 1968. Within nineteen months, the new government of Portugal granted independence to Angola. Under this system, the civil war was fought among the three liberation movements and lasted almost three decades. In February 2002, Jonas Savimbi was trapped and killed near the border with Zambia. Six weeks later, the new UNITA leaders signed a peace agreement that has lasted up to 2020.

My Parents, 1930s and Beyond

My father was about twenty years older than my mother. Before their marriage, my father had a son, whom none of us children knew. I am not sure whether he died before my father married my mom or just disappeared. I don't know whether my father or my mom had formal schooling, but I know my father knew how to read and write. Once a week, my father led a worship service, in which he preached in Cavango mission. (See picture in the middle of the book.) I remember him preaching Mathew 25:31–33. This sermon got him into trouble. His congregation was upset because he had metaphorically called them "Sheep and Goats." My mom could write her name, read the Bible well, and sing the hymns. My father never called my mom by her name unless he told a story about her. He called her "*amunu*" ("ahmoo'noo"), which means a "person" in the Umbundu language. This conveyed respect.

My father was a carpenter and worked at the Bunjei mission station. He was the only breadwinner for the family. He made sure nobody went hungry and covered all the household expenses. He worked from Monday through Friday. On Saturdays, he helped my mom in whatever capacity she needed.

Like many mothers, my mom stayed home and prepared the food for all of us. She kept the house very well and clean. Her daily activities included working in her field. Mornings on the plateau were usually cold when she got up as the sun rose about six o'clock. She threw a few grains of corn to the chickens and gave breakfast to her family. She put the youngest child on her back, took her basket, put her hoe and other things in it, and started for the field about six miles from the house. Toddlers walked along beside her. She worked the field with a hoe having two short handles. This meant leaning over at a right or left angle, giving the child on the back a bumpy ride as she tilled with the hoe. She planted the corn, dropping the kernels on the ridges and covering them by quick strokes of the hoe. In between the ridges of corn, she planted beans whose combination gave the proper diet to the family—corn and beans. Though farmers had not discovered this scientifically, corn and beans planted together provided nitrogen for all the plants. Among the corn and beans, she sparingly planted squash whose large leaves shaded the ground, thus preserving moisture from the sunny heat around the corn and bean roots. My father built a grass hut in the field which was used as a shelter from rain, a place for drying beans and corn and a place for youngsters to play. About four or five o'clock, she filled her basket with the ripe produce to take home. Besides the food, she piled the basket high with firewood and headed home with her youngsters. When she got home, she stirred up the fire on the floor in the middle of the kitchen and put on two earthenware pots which she had made. The larger pot was for the cornmeal mush, *pirao* ("peerah'umm"). The smaller was for whatever relish she had chosen to go with the mush-beans, greens, or fish or meat. This relish was called *ombelela and was* very tasty.

My Early Experiences and Education

Childhood in Bunjei Mission, 1942

In May 1942, I was born at our house in Bunjei mission station about 160 kilometers from the city of Nova Lisboa (Huambo), Angola. All of us were born at home with the help of a neighbor lady, as was the normal practice for that time. I was the third, so far the only boy, born to Joao (ʒuˈɐw) Pintar and Joana (ʒuˈɐna) Camana. Afterward, four more children were born. Sadly, two girls at the ages of three and five died just two weeks apart of an unknown disease. The next child born, a boy, also died at the age of two from malaria complications. At that time in Angola, many children died from various diseases, lack of vaccines, malnutrition, and poor sanitation.

We were baptized in a church as babies by sprinkling. We had godparents who took responsibilities like parents. Unfortunately, I don't remember my godparents because we moved away from Bunjei mission. Our parents took us to Sunday school. No one could take Communion until learning the catechism and being confirmed. We learned songs in Portuguese including "Jesus Loves Me, This I Know" ("Cristo Tem Amor Por Mim") and "Welcome, Children" ("Vinde Meninos").

My parents had a big house (in perspective) made of adobe and the roof covered with thatched (dry straws) material. The house was surrounded by lots of fruit trees, including oranges, bananas, tangerines, mangoes, lemons, guavas, *loquats* (*nesperas* in Portuguese), and others. Also my parents had a vegetable garden and a farm six miles away from the house. All the food we ate came from either the

26

farm or the garden. They grew wheat along the creeks. My sisters and I took turns to shew the birds away by shouting at them to prevent their eating the wheat. I would shout, shout, and shout until they went away. My parents also raised chickens and hogs. My father killed hogs to sell the meat to neighbors and provide some for the family. Sometimes, they killed a chicken either to honor a guest or to celebrate a holiday (Christmas, New Year's Day, or a birthday). They fed corn to the chickens and corn bran to the pigs.

We had two meals a day, breakfast and dinner. At breakfast, my parents prepared grits (broken dry corn grains) or *pirao* (*peerah'umm*), which was made of corn/cassava flour mixed in boiling water. At dinner, we ate pirao with a soup made of greens or with cooked beans. I was a good eater and was not a picky eater. Of course, kids ate whatever the parents prepared for them. Each person in the house had a plate, a fork, a spoon, and a cup to use. I was very selfish. I demanded that my parents not allow others to use my plate or utensils. My parents didn't have any extras sets of these for guests. I would cry without stopping until my demands were met. I think I was spoiled by being the only boy.

We had several holidays. Besides Christmas, New Year's Day, and Easter, we had Portuguese national holidays, such as Portugal Independence Day, the President Day (Carmona and Salazar), the Luis de Camoes (the Portuguese poet who wrote "The Lusiadas"), and others that I don't recall. Christians presented a drama of the birth of Christ on Christmas Eve. There was no Santa Claus and no gifts to exchange. On New Year's Eve, kids went out singing ritual songs ["Beta (behtta), beta, beta, beta calamba ('cahlahm'bah') beta..."], dancing, playing drums, hand cymbals, shakers, hand bells, and whistles. They went door to door. People gave them dry foods such as beans, corn, rice, corn flour, etc. It looked like trick-or-treat at Halloween in the United States. On Christmas and New Year's Day, my parents usually prepared a big meal of potatoes, beans, and pork all cooked together in a big pan (called *ochipikila* in the Umbundu language).

At age three to six, I built playhouses in the sandy soil and played with dolls with my neighbor girl named Balbina ("Bahlbee'nah"). I played hide-and-seek with her too. Also, I enjoyed pushing a bicycle rim with a wooden stick and riding a wooden scooter.

I slept with my parents in the same bed until age four or five. I had lots of dreams while I was sleeping. I fantasized flying like a kite. Most of my dreams had me flying out and over the mountains and a cliff. All of a sudden, I would fall into the valley. Then I would fearfully wake up, sit up in the bed, and shout. My parents would ask me, "What happened?" After holding me, they would rock me for a little while. Then they would put me back in bed and rub my tummy or my back until I was asleep.

At an early age, I was interested in becoming a shoemaker when I grew up. One of our neighbors was a shoemaker whom I called "Uncle" Adam (in Angolan tradition all the elders are called uncles and aunties). He made his own very special shoes. He was very handsome, careful about his clothes, and always wore suits to church. He would enter the sanctuary after the first hymn when everyone else was seated. He would walk slowly to the front pew. His very well-polished shoes squeaked while he walked down the aisle. Then he would take his handkerchief from his pocket, carefully unfold it, place on the pew, and sit on it. People looked at each other with astonishment and wonderment. Uncle Adam was my hero, and he inspired me very much. Years later, when I carefully read the Bible, I thought Uncle Adam's actions were similar to Jesus telling His disciples about hypocrisies, "Be careful not to practice your righteousness in front of others to be seen by them. If you do, you will have no reward from your Father in heaven" (Matthew 6:1 NIV). Nevertheless, I was very fascinated by Uncle Adam, but my fantasy of becoming a shoemaker was never fulfilled!

My oldest sisters, Joaquina and Julieta, were rivals. Joaquina, the firstborn, was about five feet tall, petite, and more outspoken than Julieta. Julieta, the second born, was five feet and five inches tall and a little heavier. Joaquina didn't like to be with her sister in public because people thought Julieta was older and gave her more attention. Joaquina hated this perceived disrespect. She would tell Julieta, "Stay behind and far from me!" No matter how our parents tried to change this behavior, Joaquina never changed. Julieta eventually tolerated her and lived with the situation.

Afflicted by smallpox, 1949

At the age of seven, I was afflicted by severe smallpox. I had blisters all over my body. A few little deep scars are still very conspicuous on my face. Sometimes, people wonder without asking what happened to me to cause the scars. Some of my grandchildren, when they were little, curiously asked me, "What are those little scars, and what happened to you, Grandpa?" Fortunately, I survived that deadly disease. I don't remember how my parents took care of me, because I was unconscious for about three months. But I do vividly remember how weak I was during the long recovery. My parents told me that every morning for about four months, they would boil water and mix corn bran (made from the tough outer layer of whole kernel corn) with the hot water. Then they would rub the lukewarm mixture on my entire body. Afterward, they would take me outside to dry my skin. The full treatment and recovery took almost two years. I was told there was no vaccine against smallpox; therefore, many children died of serious complications, including dehydration, pneumonia, bleeding problems, and the inflammation of the brain (encephalitis, cerebellar ataxia). I missed school for two years. Later, I will write of how missing school has affected my official date and place of birth.

Dad looking for work, 1951

In Bunjei mission, construction work was scarce. My father traveled to the new Leprosarium mission station in Cavango, where jobs were available. The Leprosarium Hospital treated patients with leprosy. As a carpenter, he and others built houses for workers and patients. He found a good job and decided to move there on a temporary basis. Not wanting to move alone, he asked me to go with him. In July 1951, we traveled on foot for a day and a half. We spent a night at one of the villages along the way. People were very hospitable, providing food and a place to sleep to anyone who came to their homes. At the age of nine, I found it difficult to trek a full day and a half for the first time in my life. Moreover, this was only about two years after I had recovered from smallpox. I was still physically traumatized by the illness.

My father liked his job, and I made new friends. He enrolled me in the first grade as a new starter. Since I missed two years due to the illness, the school leaders decided to decrease my age by two years to match the usual age of the grade level. They gave me a new official birth certificate stating that I was born in 1944, rather than 1942. Also they changed the location of my birth from Bunjei, district of Galangue and province of Huila, to Cavango, district and province of Huambo. I kept this year of birth and the birth location until the present time (2020). This age change even caused me to work two extra years before retiring with equal benefits.

Cavango Mission Station, 1952

In June 1952, my father went back to Bunjei, sold his property, and moved my mom and two sisters to Cavango. I didn't go with them to Bunjei, because I was in school. I was glad to avoid the torture of walking so far again. I stayed with one of the neighbors. At the time of the move, my oldest sister, Joaquina, was in her early twenties and had already moved out of the household. While at Means School (girls' school) in Dondi, she met a boy who was also from Bunjei. He was studying at the Currie Institute (boys' school) about five miles from her school. After a year of dating, they had married, and she no longer lived with us but would visit sometimes.

Life in Cavango

Starting at the age of ten, I studied the catechism for a year. I learned the leadership structure, baptism, Communion, some Bible stories, and the books of the Bible. Then I was orally tested by deacons and elders sitting around a table. After passing the test, I was confirmed. I could officially participate in communion. Besides teaching the Ten Commandments, the early church prohibited drinking alcohol, smoking cigarettes, and dancing at parties. Sometimes, the leaders of the church set extreme rules. I remember at the age of sixteen, while on vacation, the youths celebrated someone's birthday and danced all night. The elders of the church heard about the dancing and called us to a meeting. They decided to suspend us for one semester. After learning about the situation, the missionaries intervened, causing us to not be suspended because of one night of simple dancing. They said the youths needed entertainment once in a while.

Again in Cavango and like many residents, my dad and mom had a big garden around the house and a farm about six miles away. They grew vegetables, including tomatoes, kale, lettuces, carrots, cabbage, and many more. They grew most of the corn, beans, cassava, and wheat on the farm. My dad got up early to plant or pull weeds from the garden before he went to work. Sometimes, he got me up very early to help him. However, normally, I was not a happy camper, leaving my warm bed! But I could not openly complain. My father was a disciplinarian. He was committed and loyal to his family and to his job. He was known as an industrious person, and I learned so much from him, so that later, I was also a diligent worker on whatever task I did. My dad left me a legacy of carpentry and being a hard worker, among other characteristics. He didn't have much money, but his earnings from work and farming were used to feed and educate his children.

Ana's parents valued education like mine. My dad vowed all his children should finish middle school (*quarta classe*—fourth-grade level), which was the normal highest level needed to get a good job. Many parents didn't value education, especially for girls. They considered girls as helpers for their mothers until eventually getting married. My dad's coworkers told him to invest his money in buying cattle and equipment to farm effectively and get rich. My father refused to accept their advice. He would rather go broke and have his children educated. My oldest and youngest sisters went to Means School (girls' school), and I went to Currie Institute (boys' school) in Dondi. I will mention these schools in more detail later. The boys could find jobs, get married, and start a family. At that time, girls didn't work outside the homes. My parents made sure that we were treated well and equally. There was no favoritism. This kept us very strong and united as a family. Later, Ana and I continued this strength in our family.

I was enrolled in the elementary school in Cavango until the second grade. My teacher's name was Israel Canjila. He was very tall and slim. As a child, I thought he was very tall, but when I became an adult, I realized he was of average height. I remember being in trouble only one time. He sent me to his house to deliver a message to his wife, Dona Miquelina. The Portuguese title "Dona" was used for an adult woman, whether married or single. It was usually used with the first name of a woman. There were no telephones. Therefore, communication was mainly just mouth to mouth. I don't remember his message, but I do remember the chastisement I got from not using the right way of addressing elders. As a tradition, a young person never calls an older person by his/her first or last name. He uses "Uncle" for a man or "Auntie" for a woman. After I delivered the message to my teacher's wife, I returned to the classroom. The teacher asked me what his wife had said. I forgot and I said, "Your wife…" instead of "Auntie or Dona…" What trouble I caused! He lectured me for a few minutes and told me to kneel down at a corner on the hard floor of the classroom and stay there for almost an hour. I learned my lesson.

Siblings, 1953

After losing the two daughters in Bunjei, my parents were very happy to welcome a baby boy in 1953. They named him Justino. Justino was a very beautiful baby, and I loved him so much. I didn't love him just because he was handsome but also because he was my only brother. He had light skin. I was told by my grandpa Chimbanda Chissima that my mom's father had very light skin. My mom and his brother, Celestino, had light skin. The dominant gene from my mom transmitted it to all my siblings, except to my oldest sister. She got that gene from our dad, so they were the darkest of the family. By the way, all our first names in the family started with *J*. My father was Joao, my mom Joana, their first born Joaquina (ʒuɐkee'na), then

Julieta (ʒulieh'tta), Jose (ʒuze'), Juliana (ʒulia'na), Julia (ʒu'lia), Josefina (ʒuzɐphee'na), Justino (ʒustee'nu). My father's and mom's names were given to them when they converted to Christianity. When they were baptized, the missionaries gave them the new first names— from Cambinda to Joao Pintar and my mom from Camana to Joana Camana. I don't know why my dad didn't keep the Cambinda name.

The Cavango mission station was located along and close to the Cuvango River. This river caused lots of mosquitoes during the rainy seasons. Unfortunately, my brother Justino got acute malaria and developed high fevers that took his life in 1955 at the age of two. This was another big loss in the family. My parents lost three of their seven children under the age of six, with me being their only surviving son.

Lutamo-Dondi and Currie Institute 1955–1961

Hardships, 1955

In 1955, I was in my last school year in Cavango. Being a good student, I was sent with six other students to the Lutamo-Dondi mission station to study and take the test for the next level, the third grade. The tests were written by the Portuguese. The inspectors/teachers who tested us were white Portuguese either from the town of Bela Vista close by Dondi or from the city of Nova Lisboa, the capital city of Huambo district. I was eleven years old (official age) when we walked to Dondi. We needed to be there at least six weeks to study and take practice tests before the real exams. My mom packed my little bag with basic food (flour, dry leaves, salt, little oil, dry beans). My father gave me a little cash. It took us two days to walk to the mission. Again, the people in the villages where we spent nights along our journey were very hospitable. They provided food and a place to sleep. Lutamo-Dondi mission station was about one hundred miles from Cavango mission. Among all students who went to study for the exams, we were the most distant ones coming from villages. Normally, others went to their home villages to get food every weekend. (Ana Isabel and her family lived about thirty miles from Lutamo-Dondi—a one-day walking distance). We stayed at the place called "*zincos*" (aluminum). The buildings were built with hard aluminum layers. The buildings were extremely cold at night but very hot during the days. Also, noisy rain on the roofs made sleep almost impossible.

Our food from home was normally finished within two weeks. It was a struggle to survive without sufficient food. The classes were intensive. We needed to be in the class room at 8:00 a.m. until 4:00 p.m. with a one-hour break for lunch. After classes, we tried to find someone who needed work done so we could earn some much-needed money. We had to wait until Saturday mornings to buy food in the town of Bela Vista about four miles one way. Besides the corn flour and the dry salt fish, we bought a rustic hard bread (*boroa* in Portuguese) and sugar. We were so hungry that when we crossed the little creek we could not wait. We dipped the pieces of bread in the water, sprinkled sugar on them, and swiftly ate them! "Hmm, hmm, hmm, yummy, delicious!" we eagerly said. To save food, we had just one meal a day. Normally, the food we bought was finished by Wednesdays. On Thursdays and Fridays, we ate wild guavas and other exotic fruits, loquats (nesperas—small and sweet fruit, bigger than an olive). God provided, like He did for the people of Israel in the desert eating manna and quail. "The Lord said to Moses, 'I will rain down bread from heaven for you. The people are to go out each day and gather enough for that day'" (Exodus 16:4 NIV).

A few days before the tests, I had very severe diarrhea. I could not go out to look for a work to make money for food, because I was extremely sick. It was doubtful that any food would have helped me, anyway!

The time arrived to take exams. The written test consisted of an inspector/teacher writing the questions on a blackboard with each student writing answers. I remember reading the questions with impaired vision. My very severe diarrhea, lack of food, and dehydration caused a temporary problem with my vision. I would squint my eyes and then open them widely to read the question and quickly write the answer because my eyes would turn blurry in few seconds. I continued this process until I finished the test. "He gives strength to the weary and increases the power of the weak" (Isaiah 40:29 NIV) I was informed that I had passed.

Within a few days, the oral test would begin. However, in the meantime, it seemed that an angel visited. He was a friend named Manuel Savihemba who worked at a hospital laboratory in Dondi. He was surprised to see my health conditions. The following day, he came back and brought some medicine and a little food. After taking the medicine, my diarrhea stopped, and I started feeling much better. I went into the oral exam with some strength and passed it easily. "Brother" Savihemba was my angelic savior!

School at Lutamo-Dondi, 1956

In 1956, I started school in Lutamo-Dondi. Since I was a very dedicated and diligent student, my third grade was exceptional, and I passed the class with honors.

In my fourth and the last grade in Lutamo, I kept my momentum in my studies. People called me "genius" and said my last name "Chimbanda" was a true meaning of who I was. Chimbanda means an herbal doctor (*curandeiro* in Portuguese—healer). My dream was that someday I would become a physician to match the name. I was not a genius, but I worked very hard and took my studies very seriously. Like some other students, I would often wake up about 5:00 a.m. and go to an isolated area. I would talk loudly to memorize geography, history (Portuguese, not Angolan), human and botany science, or Bible verses in Umbundu language. In the evening, to get away from people, I would go to the same place to read loudly and memorize. Somehow, I was learning much better by reading loudly.

I only stayed in my room when I studied math with a kerosene light. Normally, this light released fumes and smelled like diesel which was unhealthy. I did not have a girlfriend, because I needed to focus on studies and I was shy. I was number one in our graduating class and considered as valedictorian in academics and in Bible. At the commencement, I delivered the speech of farewell. I felt my life changed with all these successes despite the many challenges. God was good to me.

School vacation

I only went home to see my parents in the summer. Besides spending time with them, I worked for the missionaries in the gardens and kitchens. The missionaries from Canada and the United States were very generous to me paying more than other people. This helped me save money for the following school year.

I remember one time there was a need for someone to go to the town of Bela Vista (a distance about a hundred-mile, or 160-kilometer, round trip) to take and bring the mail. This was the only way of sending and receiving mail by "pony express." They did not use a pony but a person and his bicycle. The regularly assigned person was sick, so they asked me to do it. At the age of thirteen or fourteen, I accepted the responsibility and left home at 6:00 a.m. I pedaled fast, so the trip took only one day. It was a sunny and warm day. On the way back, I noticed my water bottle was empty. There were no rivers or creeks along the road. At one point, I was very thirsty after I ate a piece of bread and a banana, the only food I had with me. As I was desperate, I suddenly saw a puddle of standing water on the road since it had rained the night before. Without hesitation, I laid my bike on the side of the road, stooped, and leaned toward the spot. When I saw some worms swimming back and forth, I thought for a few seconds. I was so thirsty that the worms did not stop me from drinking that water. Again, the good Lord provided me with water to quench my thirst. With joy, whistling and thankfulness, I continued pedaling my bike "on the road again!" I was thankful to God that I did not become ill.

Traveling to Dondi

While going back and forth between Lutamo-Dondi and Cavango for school, our group had to spend at least one night at a village. One night, we were hosted by a village chief, and he gave us a room in one of his compounds. Normally, the host would provide mats; and we would use our own blankets, sheets, or cloths to cover ourselves. The weather was good, and the temperature was comfortable enough to sleep without using heavy covers. Unfortunately, the room was not clean. The floor was full of parasites, especially ticks (small spiderlike arachnids that bite to fasten themselves onto the skin and suck the blood). As I am writing this, I have goose bumps. We were bitten all that long night. A week after I got home, I ran high fevers. I could not eat or drink anything but vomited constantly. In a couple of days, I lost weight and became dehydrated. My parents took me to the hospital where I tested positive for Lyme disease. They gave me a high dose of antibiotics. After a couple of weeks, I was completely healed, thanks again to God!

The Hockersmiths, 1958

To get facts from greatly appreciated missionaries, I asked Darrell and Barb Hockersmith to write of their experiences. They became close friends of ours. They had lived close to the Angolans for many, many years. The gracious expression of their journey of life in Southern Africa is quoted below:

> In October 1956 Darrell & Barbara Hockersmith with our two sons, David and John Mark left the USA for language study in Portugal (Stephen [third baby born in Portugal]). Then we arrived (with our three sons) in Angola in January 1958 and at the Cavango Leprosarium (we had a few months first at Catota). We replaced Dr. Regina Pearson who had to leave Cavango due to serious illness.
>
> Our son Stephen was just three years old when he climbed on two stools and found on the top shelf of the Brown's medicine cabinet (fellow missionaries, with the Brown's little boy about the same age) above the sink in their bathroom, the bottle of sugar-coated tablets for the treatment of malaria. Barb was able to put a tube into Stephen's stomach and retrieved some of the

tablets; however, enough had already entered his blood stream that he died very quickly. In the meantime, the Brown's rushed their little boy to Dondi hospital (about 100 miles) where his stomach was washed out, but obviously he had not swallowed as many (or if any) tablets and he was okay, thankfully. Jose (I) attended the funeral and he remembered the heavy rain came down like cats & dogs with a rainbow appearing in the sky.

The Hockersmiths were at Cavango where during vacations I worked for them for high wages. This was important for my schooling since my dad was not earning much from his job. They continued writing,

We were in Angola at the beginning of the colonial war in 1961; however, we left for the USA as we had already been away for five years and the mission policy those years was to return to the States for a year for what is now called "Home Assignment." Our fourth son was born in Michigan November of 1961. When we were ready to return to Angola the war was raging and the government would not allow us to return. We then went to what is now Zambia where we served for 5 1/2 years.

After one year in the USA, when we applied to return to Angola, we were granted a return visa in 1972, again returning to Cavango where we worked with Dr. Bob Foster until early 1976. The civil war had started in 1975 and we had to evacuate in early 1976 traveling by car with Dr. Foster (his family was already back in the USA) south over land, escorted by South African soldiers to Namibia, on to Pretoria by military plane and left Johannesburg, South Africa via Brazil and back to the States. Our youngest son, Paul, had been evacuated in 1975 on the last American flight from Huambo back to the USA to live with his eldest brother, Dave & Nancy, in Zion, IL as he was in the 9th grade and needed to be in school.

Though we left Angola via the back door, we were allowed once again through the front door to return to Angola in 1977; but due to the raging civil war (Cavango had been destroyed), we lived in Lubango for the remaining years of our overseas missionary service (14 years), retiring from active missionary service in Angola July 1991, just a few weeks after the civil war ended.

Back in the USA we served our Mission in Ft Mill, South Carolina as Candidate Director & secretary for three years after which we officially retired from the Mission in September 1995.

Not knowing where we wanted to make "home," we came to Colorado Springs, CO where son Paul and family were living. Paul needed help in their business, Krafted Homes, Inc., so Darrell helped Paul and we've never moved from Colorado—just from Colorado Springs, to Monument (December 12, 2015) where a few years ago Paul had built an apartment on to their home for us. We lived in our own home on Silent Rain Dr. for twenty years, but at our age, felt it was now time to be nearer Paul & family when we could help make the move.

God has guided us in marvelous ways and continues to meet our needs all these many, many years and we thank Him for being allowed to serve the people of Angola. It was hard leaving Angola and our friends there, but coming to know and fellowship with our dear Angolan friends, Jose & Ana Chimbanda in the USA is something we deeply thank God for, love them and cherish their love and friendship.

It's incredible all that Jose & Ana have been through with their family over many years, yet their strong faith and trust in God has never left them. What a testimony you are to God's grace and love and we thank God for knowing you. We miss our visits with you.

The Hockersmiths endured the colonial war (started in the early '60s) and the civil war (started in 1975) in Angola. Like many missionaries who receive the call from God whether in the past, in the present or in the future, they all needed to possess the endurance that reminds us of the apostle Paul, being himself a missionary, talking about his sufferings and victories in his letter written to Corinth:

> We are hard pressed on every side, but not crushed; perplexed, but not in despair; persecuted, but not abandoned; struck down, but not destroyed. We always carry around in our body the death of Jesus, so that the life of Jesus may also be revealed in our body. (2 Corinthians 4:8–10 NIV)

(See picture in the middle of the book.) Our words cannot adequately express the importance of dedicated missionaries, like the Hockersmiths.

Introduction to the big city

During the time I was in the Cavango mission, I took my first trip to the big city, Nova Lisboa. Missionary Hockersmith took his family and me on a business trip. I rode on the back of the open truck. I was very impressed and fascinated with the big city, the lights on the streets, many cars moving on streets, and many people walking on the sidewalks. Every major street intersection had a policeman directing cars turning and moving quickly. The lights were flashing in the windows of stores. The gardens were very well designed with flowers blooming. There were statues of historical Portuguese heroes erected at rotundas. I was seeing God's beauty, and I was at the mountaintop! As a young and naïve boy from the village and having seen only the small towns (Bela Vista, Chinguar, and Vila Nova), I was witnessing the tall and beautiful buildings and the dynamism of the city. I concluded that the government or business companies had hired people to drive cars to cause the city to appear very busy.

In 1958, I graduated from the fourth grade with honors academically and biblically. I was admitted to Currie Institute do Dondi (the boys' school). The institution was established on October 5, 1914. It was founded by Reverend Dr. Walter T. Currie, the pioneer missionary. In 2014, about fifty thousand people came to celebrate its one hundred years—the Diamond Jubilee. The theme came from Revelation 21:5 (NIV): "I am making everything new!" The mission station had been completely destroyed by the communists during the civil war but had been rebuilt.

Teenager in Dondi

The Currie Institute and Means schools (the girls' schools) were founded by Congregational and Evangelical Canadian and American missionaries. The boys and the girls were trained to become leaders and teachers. Besides these institutions, the missionaries founded a theological seminary and a hospital to train pastors and nurses/technicians (x-ray and phlebotomy). They built a few mission stations in the center of Angola, such as Lutamo-Dondi, Bailundo, Chileso, Camundongo, Chissamba, Elende, and Bunjei, where students were graduated after finishing middle school (quarta classe). Later, when I came to United States as a student in 1975, I worshiped at the Congregational Plymouth Church in a suburb of Washington, DC. We were told that the Bunjei mission station was built with the funds raised by missionaries who attended that church. After quarta classe, the students had to pass biblical and academic tests to qualify to pursue their education in any of the above institutions.

In the 1950s, the missionaries also founded a technical and academic school close to Currie Institute where they hired white Portuguese teachers to educate students at a high academic level. One had to have a high cumulative grade average from prior education and pass the placement test to enter that school. I was blessed that I had completed those levels and qualified to enter the technical and academic school. A student had to finish four years at the Currie Institute or Means School to graduate. Graduates were ready to teach or to be trained as clergy at the Theological Emmanuel Seminar or be trained as health professions at the Dondi Hospital. I had two years at the Currie Institute and then moved to the technical and academic school for two more years, totaling the four years necessary to graduate from both institute and technical and academic schools. The teachers were Dr. Luis Ribeiro, known by the nickname "Cambinga," who taught Portuguese language and history; Dr. Viriato da Silva, who taught general science (human, botany, geography, and math); and Joao Gomes, who taught art and design. Dr. Cambinga taught me the Portuguese language which involved the language structure, grammar, and writing compositions so well that writing in Portuguese language has been my forte. Certainly, this writing helped me when I learned the English language at universities, especially in writing. My English compositions earned good grades, As and Bs. It has been said that when one can master his first language well, he can also master his second language well.

The Currie Institute and Means School were other levels of education and social life. These were protestant with students from all evangelical and congregational mission stations, predominantly from the central part of Angola. These institutions were highly respected and prestigious schools, similar to the top ranked USA universities, like Yale, Harvard, Colombia, Duke, and Princeton. The tuition, room, and board costs were very reasonable. Most of the church and political leaders were educated by these institutions, including Jonas Savimbi, the president of UNITA. I estimate that 75 percent of the educated men and women were Protestants who were educated at the

evangelical and congregational missions. The majority of the educated black Angolans went through those two institutions. Kudos to
American and Canadian missionaries who did extraordinary work
educating the Angolans! The Portuguese government was based on
Catholicism and the government officials were not interested in educating Angolan natives.

Rituals in Currie Institute

There were rigid regulations and rituals to follow in Currie
Institute. Any who broke any of the rules could be punished. The
first-year students were called "*caloiros*" as freshmen. A caloiro had
to always wear a jacket and long pants to go outside and a bow tie
to go to the cafeteria even in the hot and steaming summer heat. I
suppose the reasoning was to prepare students to wear formal clothes
appropriate to their profession. I remember later when I was working
as a government civil servant, I had to wear a tie and a jacket, and
they were no longer uncomfortable to me. A caloiro had to call the
"elders," "*mano*" (old brother) with lots of respect. All the caloiros
lined up for meals and were the last to enter the cafeteria. They had
to be "initiated" like in fraternities and sororities in the United States
to move to the second year called "*cipaio*" as sophomores. During
this transition, there was much celebration of their freedom from the
freshmen rituals and strict submissiveness.

Cipaios, the second level, had no dress code except on Sundays,
when ties and jackets were required for everybody, especially when
going to church. They wore any colors except the black jackets and
white pants reserved for the next level. This freedom permitted a
cipaio to call anybody by their first name, or brother-in-law or cousin
based on the relationship among the mission stations. For instance,
coming from Dondi mission, I would call "cousin" any person from
Camundongo and Chissamba, and "brother-in-law" anyone from
Elende, Chilesso, Bailundo, and Bunjei missions.

In the third year, the students were named "*utima*" (the heart of
the institution) as juniors. Sometimes, they conducted the meetings
between the caloiros and the cipaios. They oversaw the caloiros and

assured that they were treated fairly. On Sundays, they wore black jackets and white pants. Also they were allowed to entertain and make announcements at the meals during the week.

The highest echelon was the fourth-year students named "*minhocas,*" "worms" (flexible) who were seniors. They were highly respected, and they could counsel/advise and run all the meetings. On Sundays, they wore white suits with ties or bow ties. They could be liturgists or preachers in the worships. This training prepared them to face the real world. During the Sunday meals, they were the only entertainers and announcers.

In the cafeteria, before the food was served, we sang a blessing song in Portuguese, like "Que Vista Amavel," "Gracas Te Damos Oh Senhor," or, in Umbundu, "Pandu ku Suku Tate," meaning "Be Present at Our Table, Oh Lord..." or "Thanks be to God..."

I didn't know exactly how the Means School (girl's school) conducted their rituals. However, I know the girls in all levels wore white dresses on Sundays.

Every Sunday morning, the girls came from their school to Currie Institute and worshiped with the boys. Boys and girls were thrilled to meet each other, whether to see the village fellows, encounter someone for a date, or just "feast their eyes" on the opposite sex. There were no telephones, so the communication was mainly by writing letters. I was focused on studies and too shy to date anyone. I had interest in some beautiful girls, but I was not confident enough to approach them. The students selected from the institute and the Means schools went to the technical and academic school where the boys and girls studied together in their classes. Therefore, boys and girls enjoyed being together on all days except Saturdays.

The students from the boy and girl schools met once a month on a Saturday afternoon in an open field at Currie Institute for entertainment. There was a missionary, named Sir Malcolm, known by a nickname in Umbundu language "Elengue." *Elengue* means "stylist" or "physically fit." He was in charge of physical education and the music equipment. Besides the square dancing, there were a few games and other events. They made teams to compete with each other. One of the games was running or jumping with both legs in a big bag.

Whoever got to a mark first would win a prize. Also there were teams competing to run on a track. I was average in these various skills, with my future competitive running abilities not yet evident. These were great and enjoyable Saturday afternoons for students. Everyone looked forward to participating.

The male and female seniors prepared farewell songs for the commencement. A well-known song was "Kuende Po A Kutatu, Vonjila Yove." It means "Goodbye, Kutatu, Your Way Out." "Kutatu" was the name of the river that was between Currie Institute and Means School. On the big holidays, special events, and every Sunday, girls would make two lines, like in the military to walk across the bridge heading to Currie Institute to meet the boys. On a few occasions, the boys would cross the river heading to Means School to meet the girls. The River Kutatu was pivotal to all who went to those institutions.

Curriculum

At the Currie Institute, we learned academic subjects like math, science, Portuguese history, geography, music, and the Bible. Also we had hands-on art classes involving carpentry, masonry, tailoring, agriculture, and metallurgy. Every six weeks, students rotated among the various subjects. I got an award in the carpentry class. I believe the strong bonds with my dad's profession helped. Later in Cavango, I built an annex to my parents' home, where I could stay during vacations. Also I built a dining table for my room. While I was in the tailoring class, I learned how to cut material and sew my own pants. Thus, I no longer had to buy clothing of the colors required for different levels and activities. At the Means School, the girls studied cooking, crocheting, knitting, sewing, quilting, and needle pointing. In 1962, I graduated from the Currie Institute (see pictures at the end of the book). As of 2020, from the group picture, there are only two of the known survivors.

Lifetime of Enjoying Music

I have loved to sing since childhood. It has always been an amazing source of enjoyment and of expressing my faith in God. Early successes in singing and learning more about music have been very meaningful throughout my life. Music has provided relief from stress. It was something that my family could enjoy together. It is hard to find words suitable to tell of the feelings that good music provides. It is difficult to imagine anyone not being moved by hearing "I'll Fly Away" like my faith promises in my future or "Lord, Listen to Your Children Praying"; that something may happen to you when you kneel and pray. Some of the earliest and best memories of my sisters involved music.

Introduction to Music

When I went to Currie Institute of Dondi in the late 1950s, I was interested in learning how to play the piano. Unfortunately, there were no public lessons given at that time. However, there was an untuned piano in one of the classrooms in the church building. Normally, after finishing my homework at about 10:00 p.m., I went to that room and played by ear. I locked myself in for two to three hours, familiarized myself with the piano, and learned its keyboard. I put my fingers on the keyboard and was able to follow the notes—do, re, mi, fa, sol, la, ti, do. Eureka! I was proud of myself! By knowing how to do the solfeggio, by curiosity, I discovered the piano keys equivalent to the music notes.

I was fascinated with the sounds. Sometimes, the security guard would hear the piano and tell me that I was not supposed to be in the room that late. Interacting with a keyboard never became monotonous to me. This reminds me of when I later did computer programming for many hours.

I knew the song from the evangelical hymn in Umbundu titled "Yesu Eye Ekamba Lietu"; in English titled "What a Friend We Have in Jesus" with one flat. I would play it on the keyboard, and then I would match the piano key with the written music in the book. I did this for all the voices. Eureka! I tried to play all the familiar songs in one flat, first with one hand and then with both hands. However, I did not have any concept of positioning the fingers. As long as I could spread my fingers and play both notes, I was okay. Eventually, I was able to play all the music written in flats and change the sharps into flats. My music repertoire grew as I played more and more.

When I was in Nova Lisboa (Huambo), studying at the Institute of Commerce and Engineering in early 1960s, I was invited to accompany a white lady organist in playing a piano in worship at a Baptist Church. We made a good musical team although I struggled and sometimes, even paused, playing some songs in sharps and then had to catch up with her. We played together for more than a year.

To add to my musical and carpentry repertoire, I built a guitar and taught myself to play some simple folklore songs. Pursuing my passion in music, I have sung with a choir or solos at all the churches I have attended. Throughout the years, I occasionally felt very emotional and sometimes had goose bumps when I heard my favorite songs performed by a choir, quartet, or soloist.

Moved to Nova Lisboa, 1961

I moved to the big city of Nova Lisboa. Students who graduated from the technical and academic school in Dondi were qualified to be integrated into a Portuguese education. They could go either to a commercial and industrial institute or to a nacional liceu (post high school) in the city of Nova Lisboa (now Huambo). I chose the commercial and industrial institute, where I majored in accounting. This was the only Portuguese educational institution in Angola. Besides in the city of Nova Lisboa, they had nacional liceus (high schools) in the other cities. In my classroom of twenty to twenty-five students, I was the only Black student with all the others being white Portuguese. The whole institution of about six hundred students had very few Black students—maybe five to ten. It was a cultural shock for me to listen to and speak only Portuguese. Coming from the Christian environment, for the first time, I was in contact with cigarette smokers. They avoided me. It was uncomfortable, but there was nothing that

I could do to avoid it. Sometimes, I was lonely. Also I felt discrimination due to the color of my skin. This was the beginning of my mingling with White Portuguese people. All students from Currie Institute and Means School lived in a mixed dormitory, close to the liceu and to the institute. So the students could walk to their schools. After two more years of my schooling, I became eighteen years of age and was drafted into the Portuguese army. Unfortunately, I still needed two more years to graduate as an accountant. This was the drafting age for males, and no one could avoid it. One had to serve in the army to find a good job in the Portuguese government. Private organizations rarely hired Black people. The jobs were usually given to the White people.

Drafted into the Portuguese Army, 1963

As a post high school graduate, I entered the army as a militiaman. I was enrolled in the infantry. My group had two primary and essential training programs. The first was intensive physical training, including running five Ks and other physical drills, plus self-discipline and addressing everyone with respect. It was so intense that many overweight people lost several pounds in the first three weeks. We woke up at 5:00 a.m. to the sound of a trumpet. A sergeant would come to our barracks quickly to make sure everyone was awake and out of the beds. After three months of the physical training and testing, we were promoted to the first rank and became first private militiamen and did extensive classroom instruction. This required learning of the equipment related to the military and their application and platforms used on the battlefields. After six months, we had the final physical, written, and oral tests. After completion, we were promoted to a *furriel* militiaman or sergeant. (See picture in the middle of the book.) The duties and the responsibilities of the sergeant were to train and supervise junior soldiers and enlisted personnel regarding military life and personal care. A sergeant was asked to develop and mentor privates and specialists, getting them on an upwardly mobile career path while teaching them the drive and resiliency that define the army. There were many assignments. Besides being a teacher and mentor, I was a drill sergeant. Being a sergeant, I was permitted to find a residence outside the army compound.

I lived in the Capango community about three miles from the military headquarters. I rented a small room on the annex of Mr. Luis Fernando, who was a truck driver. He and his wife, Maria, had two young kids. As a Furricl Militiaman, I was highly respected by the people I met in homes or on the streets. Mr. Fernando would often leave for a day or two driving the truck away from the city. I gladly watched his family while he was away. He trusted me and gave me lots of appreciation and respect. Knowing him helped me meet my future wife.

Ana and Our Early Married Life

Meeting Ana and Getting Married, 1965

Ana Isabel Catuta was born January 16, 1947, in Sambo, district and province of Huambo. She was the last born after four siblings—Felicia, Madalena, Ilda, and Marta—to Aurelio Holongonjo and Arminda Rosa. (See picture in the middle of the book.) They were all girls. Her dad was a deacon of the Evangelical Congregational Church. Her mother was a stay-at-home-mom caring for the children like other mothers. Ana had much in common with me as she grew up. Eventually, her parents moved back to Miapia, Chiumbo, in the province of Huambo. Like my parents, Ana's dad vowed to educate his children, and all of them excelled to acquire degrees sufficient to secure good jobs. After elementary school, Ana went to Lutamo, Dondi, to continue her education. She acquired a high school diploma.

Several relatives and friends were deeply involved in the circumstances of Ana and me meeting. Her sister Marta moved to Nova Lisboa (Huambo) and married Enoc Efraim Chitonho. Ana moved there to live with them and continue her education. When Marta and Enoc moved to another city, Ana (age sixteen) got a job by succeeding Marta in Radio Broadcasting. Then Ana moved into the home of Marta's sister-in-law Laureta and husband, Porfilho Chamolonegne. This house was only about a mile from Luis Fernando with whom I had lived. Porfilho and Luis were both retired army privates and very good friends who visited one another often.

Ana was very well-known by me and many other radio listeners by her name and voice. During the day, she studied at the technical and academic school of Nova Lisboa. Her part-time work was as an anchor with a man, Lino Pessela. She dedicated music that was broadcast widely to the nation on the Umbundu-Portuguese program. It was called "O Momento do Ouvinte" ("The Time for Listeners"), which aired at 6:00 p.m. for an hour. I loved her voice and daily program, hoping I could somehow get to know her. Her voice resonated in my ears as I wondered if she could be the very special one for me.

At the beginning of 1965, I managed to meet the young and beautiful Ana Isabel Catuta, age seventeen. I introduced myself by telling about Mr. Chamolonegne and Mr. Fernando being close friends. After telling about herself, she said she needed a math tutor. I volunteered to tutor her, if she wished. Deal! My academic skills were enabling us to get to know one another. Since she worked in the evenings, sometimes I went to her work on foot and then walked her home. I often would wait for her to settle in at home, and then I would help her with algebra and trigonometry homework. We developed and increased our relationship. After a few months of dating, we got married in the city court in June of 1965.

Relocated to City of Cubal

In October 1965, I was selected and deployed at a command headquarters in the town of Cubal, District of Benguela (now a province). It was very sad for me to go far away from Ana Isabel, my wife. On the other hand, my relocation was an opportunity to learn more about hands-on leadership. Though distant geographically, I felt virtually close to her during her radio broadcasts *O Momento do Ouvinte*. I would not miss turning on the radio in my room at 6:00 p.m. Her voice seemed to me as of an angel!

Religious Wedding, 1966

We planned a church wedding. On June 25, 1966, we got religiously married at the Evangelical Church in Cubal. Besides members of Ana's family and mine, I invited several dignitaries and my military colleagues to the wedding. We had as godparents, Mr. Vigario Ecurica, the chief administrator, and his wife, Cacilda. The couple were good friends of my oldest sister, Joaquina, and her husband, Americo Mario, who lived in a nearby town. The reception was held at our godparents' house. We were going to hire a professional photographer, but one of our friends volunteered to do the job. Unfortunately, either he wanted to show off, or he didn't have enough film. He flashed at us in every move and position so that we became a little suspicious. A month passed with no pictures. After going after him, he apologized saying that he had only few pictures developed because much of the film was destroyed by water. What a disappointment! There was no way of suing and taking him to court or asking him to compensate us for the emotional damages and broken hearts. At that time, it was not popular to sue anyone. We could not dispute his negligence. We received very few pictures. We forgave him, but that damage is still lingering when we look at the few pictures we possess. (See pictures in the middle of the book.)

The Birth of Our First Son, 1966

On October 3, 1966, our first son was born at the hospital of Cubal. We named him Anibal Graca Joao Catuta Chimbanda. "Joao" was my dad's name. Traditionally, the first and the second children are named after the father's family. The third and the fourth children are named after the mother's family. Then the following children's names can be chosen by the parents. Anibal was baptized, as a baby, in the church in Cavango with godparents Mr. and Mrs. Manuel Savihemba. He had brought me medicine for diarrhea when I was very sick in Lutamo.

Patrols in Cubal

The town of Cubal is surrounded by a few hills and many native villages. The population was predominantly the Hanha Tribe. There were a few Ovimbundus (tribe) who loved to farm, but the terrain was not suitable for farming. The Hanhas primarily raised cattle (similar to the Maasai Tribe in Kenya and Tanzania), goats, and other domestic animals, including chicken and hogs. They normally lived and dressed in traditional ways by wearing two pieces of clothing, one from waist down and another on top of the body. Men and women wore lots of bracelets on their arms and legs. The number of bracelets represented the number of their cattle, their primary wealth resource. They milked cows and drank raw and soured milk.

As sergeant, I led a patrol consisting of the primeiro-cabo (corporal) and ten soldiers (privates). We went on foot into villages to search for anything suspicious against the government.

Since the late 1950s, there was increased awareness among Angolans about the people being colonized and oppressed by the Portuguese regime. The pressure of the Angolan liberation movement, operating from the neighboring countries (Zaire, Zambia, and Namibia), was heavily influential in Angola. The government had a strong secret police throughout the country. Letters, newspapers, and certain publications were censored. A few people had been arrested and interrogated for allegedly being connected to some liberation movements.

One could even be in trouble for having similar names. For instance, while I was a student at Institute Industrial and Commerce of Nova Lisboa, I was questioned for a couple of hours at the police station. They were looking for Jose Joao Chimbanda, born in district of Bie and thought I was him. I was legally born in the district of Huambo. We were totally different individuals. After a long interrogation and attempted intimidation, they possibly found some discrepancies related to the location of birth. Fortunately, they let me go and drove me back to school. I was very lucky! Those who were strongly suspected ended up in prisons. Anyway, our patrols found nothing suspicious. On a joyous note, we were given lots of live chickens and eggs by the natives. They were very generous people! Our joyous moments in Cubal didn't last long.

Deployment in Eastern Angola, 1967

In December 1966, I was selected to leave Cubal and join the infantry battalion deployment in Nova Chaves. This town is in eastern Angola in the district of Moxico, near the border with Zambia. I had to make arrangements for the care of Ana and our little baby, Anibal, while I was away on duty. Riding my motorcycle, I took them to my parents in Cavango where they lived with them for a year while I was gone. It was a hard time for Ana. During the week, she worked with her in-laws on the farm. On Sundays, she walked six miles one way to church with the baby on her back.

On December 24, 1966, I prepared to join the battalion. The separation for the first time was tough for both my family and me. Our Christmas had less joy than usual. I knew I had great parents to care for Ana and the baby, but I was still apprehensive. To make things worse, there was no way of communication except by writing letters. Sometimes, I had to wait one or two months without hearing from my family. This was nothing compared to a future time of separation to be described later.

We loaded our luggage and equipment on to the train heading to Luena City. The Caminho de Ferro de Benguela (CFB) railroad was InterRail from Lobito City port to Zaire and Zambia. Then we rode on trucks and jeeps to our new headquarters in Nova Chaves close to Luau City.

The highest-ranking officer in the Portuguese army was a captain, who commanded the battalion. Our duties were to patrol the surrounding area, in a radius of a hundred kilometers away opposing UNITA. On New Year's Day, UNITA attacked Teixeira de Sousa (now Luau). It was led by Dr. Jonas Savimbi, later the president of UNITA. Fortunately, the attacked city was about a hundred kilometers, so we were not directly involved. This was probably fortunate because I later joined UNITA and became its treasurer.

I was the leader of a regiment of twelve men—one corporal and ten privates, all relocated white soldiers from Portugal. We patrolled the location in a radius of fifty kilometers. We carried our own food, including bread and cans of tuna and sardines. Each carried a duffle bag, a rifle, and bullets; and I carried the same items plus a pistol. This was a heavy load to carry on foot! The days were overcast. It rained lightly day and night. We were always wet. My feet developed blisters from being constantly soaked in the boots. I tried changing socks, to no avail due to the continuous rain. This caused me to develop serious sinus problems. Unfortunately, I have had to endure this hardship for the rest of my life especially during winter weather.

Most of the people during the patrols smoked cigarettes to alleviate the conditions. Fortunately, I abstained from that habit though I was strongly encouraged by many of my subordinates to smoke. It helped that the captain sometimes assigned me to work in the office. Thus, I would work on scheduling and other paperwork rather than patrolling. The scheduling was not an easy task either. Some people didn't like me for scheduling them in areas they didn't like. All I could do was try to be fair to everyone.

Postdeployment Hardships, 1968

We came back to the general headquarters of Nova Lisboa. I brought my family from my parents' home. We were happy to be together again, but we had to endure poverty. We lived in Sao Joao community, near the Evangelical and Congregational Church where we worshiped. In August of 1968, I retired from the army. Coincidentally, Ana's brother-in-law, Pedro Ezequiel Chilungo (now deceased), retired from the army at the same time. To save money, we shared an apartment. It had one bedroom, an annex, two baths, a living room, and a kitchen. We occupied one bedroom and the other family slept in the annex. We shared the kitchen and the living room. It was barely sufficient for two families. Pedro and Ilda had two little boys, Miguel and Joel; and we had one. Our second child was on the way.

Both Pedro and I looked for work. We filed applications at the government offices and private organizations. I specifically applied at the Finance Services, Education, and Instituto de Veterinaria de Angola. While we were waiting, we bought small porcelain tiles on which we designed and wrote phrases for wall decorations. Some of the phrases we wrote were quotes from the Bible. We sold these at the street market. The meager profits helped us to buy food and a few other necessities. Pedro got a job at a butcher shop. He was thrilled, and at the end of the first day, he brought pork chops that our wives enjoyed cooking. We celebrated eating the good dinner! Our exuberance didn't last long. Apparently, Pedro didn't get along with his coworkers, so he decided to not go back to work the next day. One of his coworkers had apparently tried to force Pedro to do menial work. We begged and encouraged him to go back for at least for a day or two so that we could enjoy more meat. Unfortunately, he had made up his mind and would not return to the work.

The Birth of Our Second Son, 1968

On October 21, 1968, our second son was born at the Central Hospital of Huambo. We named him Azevedo Crisostomo Horacio. Horacio was my uncle's name, a first cousin of my mom. Similar to Anibal, Azevedo later dropped his second middle name. I was still unemployed when Azevedo was born.

In November, I was offered a job as an assistant administrator at the Instituto de Veterinaria de Angola. I was placed at its plant in Humpata, district of Huila, close to the city of Sa da Bandeira (now Lubango). In the meantime, Pedro got an administrative job at a hog processing plant in the town of Mungo, district of Huambo. His business butchered hogs and processed pork. Coincidentally, Pedro had found a permanent job with the same meat company where he had quit due to the difficult coworker.

The New Chapter of Life, in Humpata, 1968

The veterinary services moved us to a new location, in the town of Humpata. They packed and loaded our belongings in one of their trucks. It took eight hours in the truck to Sa da Bandeira (Lubango) city and then on to Humpata. This mission station had the responsibility of taking care of bovine animals and their health treatments. They produced crossbred animals with hybrid vigor. Also the cattle produced milk for many dairy products. The employees had lots of benefits. They gave fresh milk to employees each day. Also they butchered a cow and gave meat to each worker every weekend. My job responsibilities were data entry and bookkeeping in the accounting area. Also I had customer service and clerking responsibilities. The benefits were great, but the salary was low.

Besides the low salary, there were other inconveniences of being far from the big city. The general shopping and worshipping were about forty kilometers away from the city of Sa da Bandeira (Lubango). My German-made Zumdap motorcycle was our only transportation. The road to the city was covered with dirt and sand with lots of potholes. These conditions made it difficult to ride the motorcycle safely, especially when it rained.

When my parents came to visit us in Humpata, my dad and I decided to go to the city to shop. While riding on my motorcycle, we saw a patrolling policeman riding his horse toward us from a distance. I knew it was illegal to have a second person on a motorcycle. Therefore, I advised my dad to pretend to be sick as if I were taking him to the hospital for emergency care. He replied, "Okay." When we met the policeman, I stopped, and we dismounted. I expected Dad would be quiet and show weakness. Dad was very energetic as he immediately took off his hat and bowed down to show respect to the policeman and said, "Bom dia, senhor!" which means "Good morning, sir!" in a loud voice. Oh my, my plan didn't work! Without hesitation, the policeman gave me a violation ticket which cost me a fortune. I don't recall how much it was. Of course, my dad was always honest and truthful. This act showed me who my dad truly was. I learned the lesson—tell the truth even if it hurts or costs you something. "Then you will know the truth, and the truth will set you free" (John 8:32 NIV).

The New Transition Back to Nova Lisboa, 1969

After six months working for the company, I was listening to the early morning radio broadcast when the reception was usually best. This was the way the government notified new civil service employees. I heard my name mentioned as being hired by Finances and Services as an assistant administrator. This was the same position I had held previously, but the salary was much better. I was placed in the city of Nova Lisboa (Huambo). This was a dream come true!

First, my desire had always been to pursue my education after retiring from the army. There was no way that my dream could have been fulfilled in Humpata. Secondly, my children needed to grow up in the city where a good school system was available. Thirdly, the smaller company would have had few advancement opportunities. Fourthly and lastly, I started with better pay and with more opportunities for promotion. My previous coworkers were happy for us but sad to see us leave. They threw a farewell party for us. Throughout our lives, we participated in several bittersweet parties as we were moving onto unexplored situations.

In November 1969, we loaded our meager possessions in a rental truck and moved back to Nova Lisboa (Huambo). We rented an annex from a Portuguese businessman, Mr. Cavaco, at Bairro Benfica. It was close to the Benfica Football Club (soccer club). My motorcycle was my transportation for work about five miles each way. Ana was a stay-at-home mom caring for our two little boys.

As an assistant administrator or clerk, I did practically the same work as previously, including data entry of the receiving documents in the Accounting Department and handling correspondence. It was a lot of work for the big department of about twenty employees. I really enjoyed the environment and the prestige. It was in the Human Resources Department on the second floor of the building.

We attended the Igreja dos Peregrinos Congregational and Evangelical Church where I played the pump organ during the worship services. I also directed the choir for the church that had both Black and White worshipers. (See picture at end of the book.)

In 1971, my department selected me and two other candidates to go to the capital city of Luanda (three hundred miles away) to take promotion exams. We drove about eight hours and took the tests that included math, written essays in Portuguese, and other areas of general knowledge. It was a difficult test. After two months, we received the results that all three of us had passed the exams. We were immediately promoted to Aspirante officials. I was moved to the accounting and finances section (accounts receivable and payable). We processed checks, "titulos," for all the government employees in the district of Huambo. Also, we closed and opened the monthly accounts. People treated us as "the providers of the money." Other departments in the Finance and Services processed business and property taxes and were located on the first floor of the building. Anyone who worked at Finances and Services had special privileges as well as respect from outsiders. They tried to gain favors of employees by giving "free lunches" and invitations to restaurants. Other privileges were offered by the Center Hospital where Ana worked. Mr. Costa Pereira, chief financial officer, gave us free coupons and vouchers for drugs/medication at any pharmacy.

The Birth of Our Third Son, 1970

On March 31, 1970, our third son was born, and we named him Cicero Mario, after Ana's first cousin, Mario Chimuku. Mario came to live with Ana's parents as a young boy. As their nephew, he was reared like a son. Besides Mario, Ana's parents reared and educated three or four children for their relatives. Ana recalls their house being filled with many kids. Cicero was baptized, as a baby, in Igreja dos Peregrinos. His godparents were Mr. and Mrs. Aarao (now deceased) and Alice Cornelio.

Ana Goes Back to School, 1971

In January 1971, Ana went back to school and completed the intensive eighteen-month nursing program. After she passed the exams, she was hired as a practical nurse at the Center Hospital of Huambo. Since our income was now good, we decided to purchase our first automobile. We bought a four-door green-seat Italian-made car. We moved to Bairro de Cacilhas, the compound of government employees and were considered upper-middle-class citizens. We had finally reached a good level of comfort. We had a car; a motorcycle; and a single-family home with three bedrooms, a kitchen, a living room, and a bathroom, along with running water and electricity. Also, we had a German shepherd mixed dog, named Jolly, that stayed in the fenced backyard.

The Birth of Our Fourth Son, 1972

On April 23, 1972, our fourth son was born at the Center Hospital, and we named him Arlindo Samuel. He was named after one of Ana's Uncles, Samuel Sokuma. Like Ana's dad, Samuel was a very generous man and a great friend and supporter of Ana's dad. Arlindo was baptized, as a baby, in Igreja dos Peregrinos with his godparents also, Aarao and Alice Cornelio.

At the end of the year, the government gave bonuses (*decimo terceiro mes*) to all employees. With the extra money, Ana and I bought tailored suits for everybody. Our lives seemed better and relatively prosperous by then. This was perhaps the calm before the storm.

Seeking Household Help

Since we were both working, Ana went to her parents' village (Kimbo) and invited her eight-year-old first cousin, Emilia Gueve, to live with us and help care for our children. I went to my parents in Cavango and secured one of my relatives, seven-year-old Victoria. These girls were very helpful. They took care of the house and our two younger boys while Anibal and Azevedo were in day care. Ana hired a woman to do the laundry by hand because there were no washers and dryers.

The Birth of Our Only Daughter, 1974

On October 22, 1974, our fifth child was born at the Center Hospital. We were thrilled to have a baby daughter after four sons! We named her Clarisse Joana, after my mom, Joana. I was so involved in the political campaign for the UNITA party that Ana and I did not have time to prepare for baptizing Clarisse as a baby like her siblings. I left her at age of eleven months and two weeks when I came to the United States of America. I had no way of knowing that I would not see her or the rest of the family for almost four long years. I missed so much of her formative years. She was baptized at Eden UCC (now Eden Church) after her confirmation class.

Opportunities for Us

Close to my work building, there was a private day care center for employees who could afford it. It was primarily for predominantly rich White people. Angolan employees' kids could be accepted with some criteria. Ana and I decided to enroll Cicero (age three) in that day care since Anibal and Azevedo were already attending elementary schools. Unfortunately, it was costly, so we could afford to send only one. There was another Black child about the same age as Cicero in the same day care. Black children were only accepted because their parents were employees of Finances and Services.

Ripple Effects, 1974 and 1975

On April 25, 1974, a group of disillusioned military officers overthrew the Lisbon government in Portugal. The leader was the former governor and commander in Guinea-Bissau, General António de Spínola. The new government was intent on disowning its overseas colonies and thus gave independence to Angola in 1975. Unfortunately, independence was only the beginning of difficult times for many Angolans and Portuguese. Most Portuguese settlers fled Angola. The three nationalist movements—MPLA, FNLA, and UNITA—began jostling for power and the civil war began. I had worked as an accountant in the Payroll Department at the Public Financial Department in Nova Lisboa (Huambo) during 1970 through 1975. In May 1975, being an active member of UNITA in Huambo and having financial experience caused me to be selected to replace the party treasurer (see picture in the middle of the book), Gilberto Lutucuta, when he became the agriculture minister in the Luanda capital. My work was quite a task and an amazing experience handling thousands of dollars (USD). (See picture of Dr. J. Savimbi in the middle of the book.)

College Education Scholarship Opportunity, 1975

In August 1975, I was approached by Anacleto Ferramenta Isaias, my former classmate, friend, neighbor, and coworker at the Financial Department. He worked at the Ministry of Natural Resources in Luanda in the transitional government. He asked me whether I would consider accepting a scholarship being offered to him and a few other candidates by the Ministry of Natural Resources to study abroad. I was not sure whether I should accept the offer, since I had never left Angola and had a wife and five little children. I knew that Ana could certainly care for herself and our children while I would be gone. It was a big decision. Anacleto gave us a couple of weeks to think about it. He reminded me that he also had a family to leave behind and that our two families could watch out for one another as neighbors.

Ana and I prayed about it, and we were overwhelmed with the choices. At that moment, troops in the city carried semiautomatic rifles and shotguns conspicuously. Some civilians carried forty-caliber pistols in a discreet manner. There were already uncertainties about the future of the Angola peace settlement since there were sporadic gunshots by troops who sometimes threatened civilians. After three weeks, Anacleto came back and talked to us for an hour. Eventually, Ana and I accepted the offer. To help our family, we decided for me to move into uncharted territory—a new country and a free college education but away from my family. Our comfortable lives were about to be embroiled in more hardships to endure.

Almost Four Years of Separation, Helplessness, and Activities

My Leaving Angola, 1975

On October 1, Anacleto, the other candidates, and I prepared to leave Angola for college in the United States. The next day, Ana prepared spaghetti, but I did not have time to eat it at home. With mixed emotions, I said goodbye to Ana and our kids. With the container of food, I rushed to the airport to meet my group. I shared the food with my new friends and future classmates on the airplane. We flew from Nova Lisboa (Huambo) to Zambia to Rome and then to the United States of America. We landed at La Guardia airport in New York on October 5.

It was my first time to leave Angola and see other African countries! Riding from the airport in Lusaka, Zambia, was both fascinating and scary. It was my first time to ride in a car on the left side of the road. (Drivers in several former British colonies, including South Africa, drive on the left.) It was very confusing. I did not want to face forward to enjoy the scenery along the road. I actually put my hands over my eyes for a few minutes. We spent a few hours at the UNITA house in Zambia. I had given up my position as treasurer of UNITA because of my leaving Angola.

From Lusaka, we landed briefly in Dar es Salaam, in Tanzania. While on board, I looked through the airplane window and saw people all dressed in white and kneeling with their faces down. I asked, "Who are those people?" Someone answered, "Muslims!" Angola, having predominately Christians, had no Muslins. I had never seen or heard of them. I supposed that I had lived like a chick inside an egg. Slowly my world started "hatching" or unfolding from then forward! I was expanding my experiences drastically. In this expansion, I asked God to bless me, and I recalled the prayer of Jabez: "Oh, that you would bless me and enlarge my territory" (1 Chronicles 4:10 NIV)!

My New Life Begins in America, 1975

We twelve students were sponsored by an African American Institute, an institution of the United Nations. Kye Henderson, a former missionary in Angola, was the secretary of it. She made arrangements for our transportation and hotel reservations in New York and in Washington, DC. While in New York City, we visited the United Nations and other locations which I do not remember well because of being so overwhelmed with the new sights, people, culture, and language.

After a day, we flew from La Guardia airport to Washington, DC. We were taken to the Alban Tower Hotel in the northwest area. We stayed in the hotel for about three weeks. (See picture in the middle of the book.) One afternoon, the temperature was in the thirties, and we felt very cold. We bought coats, boots, gloves, scarves, and warm underwear for the first time in our lives. After a night of snowing, we saw that the roofs and branches of trees were covered with snow. We all wondered, "What in the world are we seeing!" Dressed in our new warm clothes, we went out to see the white stuff, whiter than flour, wet and cold like ice. When we had studied geography in Angola, we did learn about the snow that normally falls on the mountains. Also in the Portuguese hymn, I had learned a song about "Bendito Cordeiro—Alvo mais que a neve, Sim, nesse sangue lavado, Mais alvo que a neve serei" ("Blessed Lamb—Whiter than snow… that makes me white as snow. No other fount I know. Nothing but the blood of Jesus… I shall be whiter than snow"). Thus, I could relate with the snow. We touched it and even tasted it. It was beautiful. We discovered another of God's creations!

None of us knew English except Figueiredo Paulo and Aarao Cornelio (deceased) who knew some. I had studied a little British English in high school and in junior college in Angola. However, the pronunciation was completely different from what I had learned. Also if you do not use it, you lose it. With the little English we knew, we could go around, catch the city buses, and order food in restaurants. It was not easy to read the menu. The most familiar foods we knew were chicken, rice, and potatoes. Therefore, most of the time, we ordered those foods. I did not like the beans because they tasted sweet.

On our first Sunday there, we went to church. We caught the bus early that morning at the Alban Tower and transferred to another at the capitol. Eventually, we arrived at the Congregational Plymouth Church. It was an African American church that had been recommended by Mrs. Henderson, the wife of the former missionary in Angola. I later learned that it was the church that had contributed part of the funds to build Bunjei Mission at the beginning of the nineteenth century. Three of us had been born in that mission—Moises Chongolola, Aarao Cornelio (both deceased), and me. During the worship, we could sing along because most of the tunes were familiar. We were amazed by the church organist and choir. They had a huge pipe organ with multiple keyboards. When the congregation sang "Heralds of Christ," the trumpets in the organ, before each stanza and between, were amazing to us. When the choir sang with soloists at the beginning and in between, it was marvelous and awesome. I thought I was in paradise and had goose bumps. I felt that it was a mountaintop experience. I was like Peter up on the mountain with Jesus, James, and John (Matthew 17:1–4 NIV). This was basically my transfiguration! We did not understand the sermon, because of the language barriers, but the whole worship was quite an experience. Since we got to the worship late, we had introduced ourselves to the ushers at the back of the church. Aarao and Figueiredo were very helpful translating for us. During the week, we looked forward to going back to that church every Sunday. (See picture in the middle of the book.)

We settled in Arlington, Virginia, near the Arlington National Cemetery. We found an apartment for six of us including two girls, Rita Carlos and Anita Jalaimo. We went to school at the American Language Institute at Georgetown University to study English as a second language. (See picture in the middle of the book.) It was quite a trek to cross the Key Bridge on foot every morning to go to school. Sometimes, it was snowing and windy, but we had enough warm clothes to cope.

A Bird Sitting on an Empty Nest

I had wonderful things around me in the United States. However, I was like a bird on a beautiful and comfortable nest without any baby birds. I was incomplete and worried. Something pivotal was missing in my life, Ana and our children. I thought about them constantly. The Angolan civil war was rampant in the whole country, especially in Huambo where the UNITA movement had its headquarters. The MPLA movement supported by the Soviet Union with the help of Cuban troops moved gradually from Luanda, the capital city, to Nova Lisboa (Huambo) at the end of 1975. On the other hand, South Africa, which had its own colony of Namibia bordering Angola, wanted to prevent the MPLA from gaining a victory because the MPLA supported the Namibian struggle for independence as well.

At the beginning of 1976, while in Washington, DC, attending the English program, all my countrymen and I were very worried about our families. Every morning, we bought newspapers (*the New York Times, the Washington Times, the Chicago Tribune*, etc.) to update ourselves. In the evenings, we watched international news on television. All the media was bombarded by the Angolan civil war. The reporters from CBS, NBC, and ABC covered the war in detail. We especially watched the CBS Evening News by Walter Cronkite, television pioneer. He was a CBS Legend who was our favorite reporter because of his deep and strong voice. He reported, "The MPLA with the Cuban troops have been advancing to the headquarters of Jonas Savimbi." A few days later, he reported, "Today, the troops armed with sophisticated weapons bombed the city of Nova Lisboa." All of us, sitting around a TV set, went silent! In the next few days, the other media reported the same thing until they finally said, "MPLA took control of the city of Nova Lisboa, and all the UNITA troops and the population fled to the bush." Afterward, we lost all contact.

> All of us, sitting around a TV set, went silent!

There was no more news reported. The 1976 civil war took place in an era when most Angolans had no telephones. This created a gap between the people of Angola and the rest of the world. It also caused a gap among the people inside Angola. We were very devastated not knowing what was happening with our families.

English Classes and Testing Procedure

Every three months, we took the test of English as a foreign language. The required score was 550 or better to be allowed in any university. The first quarter, I only scored 400. In the second, I scored 475. In the third, I scored 520. My speaking and comprehension were still very limited. Then (Mrs.) Henderson, the student organizer for the African American Institute, decided to split us up and sent us to other universities where English as a second language classes were offered. She thought we were speaking Portuguese when not in the classrooms which was slowing our progress in learning English. She was right.

Southern Illinois University, 1976

Therefore, I went to Southern Illinois University in Carbondale for one quarter. I roomed with an American. It was quite an experience adapting to him. I was very organized. I made my bed every morning, cleaned the bathroom, and put all my clothes in a closet before leaving for classes. But when I came back in the afternoons, the room was totally disorganized, especially on my roommate's side.

One night after I went to bed, my roommate brought in some friends. I covered myself up in blankets, pretending to be asleep. I heard them saying, "He is sleeping!" They started smoking and laughing loudly. The room was full of smoke. I thought later that they may have smoked marijuana because the room smelled terrible. I had no clue about the odor, but it was really bad. I removed my blankets and coughed strongly. They quickly left the room laughing. They came back and did the same thing a few more times. Eventually, I told my roommate that I did not like their smoking in the room. It never happened again. I was very thankful that he accepted my request and considered my privacy. However, his messing up the room never stopped.

After one quarter, I scored 575. I was very happy to have exceeded the required score. I could now move on to pursue my college degree. My desire was to go to a medical school. My sponsor denied the idea by giving excuses that the scholarship only covered four years and I must return to Angola immediately after acquiring the first degree. Also she said that my having a large family would make it a long struggle to go through medical school and that it would be hard to find other scholarships. Since Angola had lots of mineral resources, we were required to study natural resources, economics, geology, or mining. I decided to major in natural resources and biology. Thus, I was sent to Ball State University, in Muncie Indiana.

My New Life at Ball State University

While in Carbondale, Illinois, I had gone to the local UCC and joined its choir. The pastor had met Pastor Fred Dare of Muncie while serving on a World Ministry Committee for the UCC. Thus, he called Fred and asked him to meet my plane and assist me upon arrival in Indiana. Wow, what a lucky break! Pastor Dare was to become my strongest supporter in my upcoming times of uncertainties, frustrations, and eventual successes.

In August, I flew to Indianapolis airport where Fred Dare and his wife, Nancy, were waiting at the gate. They drove me to their house in Muncie where I spent the night. They had four children,

Carol, Anita, Fred Jr., and Chris. Anita and Fred Jr. attended Ball State University. In the morning, Anita took me to my assigned Ball State University host family, John and Ann Campbell. I stayed with them for a week before moving into a dormitory. They were an amazing couple. They showed me many places in the Muncie area and treated me like their own child. They had three sons, one daughter, and several grandchildren. John and Ann are now deceased, but their work helping others was praiseworthy.

On Sundays, I alternated worshiping at two UCC churches. One Sunday, Anita Dare took me to the Community UCC; and the next Sunday, Don and Charlene Suldosky (both deceased) took me to their church, Eden UCC (now Eden Church). I sang in the chancellor choir at both churches.

On special occasions, friends from both churches invited me to have meals at their homes. My first Thanksgiving was hosted by Rolland Stillwagon and his wife, Judy, in their house. This was my introduction to the special Thanksgiving meal.

I lived in Shively Hall. My first roommate was not as organized as I. After a month, I requested another roommate and the resident assistant placed me with an African roommate, David Thiger, from Kenya. I was very happy with him. We shared similar African traditions and culture. There were many foreign students in our dorm. I learned a lot about other countries. Many of my fellow students were married and had left their families in their native countries, like I had.

On some Saturday nights, we would spend enjoyable times with other foreigners at a tenured African's apartment in University Family Housing. He was Jonathan Lenga, from Sierra Leone. We would eat, chat, dance, and really enjoy one another. I spent time with a friend from Mozambique, Manuel Mpinga, who was married to a White American, named Ann, who also lived in family housing. Some weekends we traveled to Chicago to visit Ann's parents. Eventually, I bought Manuel's car, a black Ford Fairlane for $150. I was proud to own and drive my first car in America. However, something was missing in my life. (See picture in the middle of the book.)

Ana Recalls Her Life during the Civil War

By word of mouth, people were telling each other that the Cubans and the MPLA troops were approaching the city of Nova Lisboa (Huambo). I was approached by my sister-in-law Juliana, who said, "Ana, my family and I are preparing to drive to the remote village of my husband very early tomorrow morning. Get your stuff, and have the kids ready. We are going to my brother-in-law's house in the outskirts of the city to spend the night." I quickly prepared our belongings and got the kids ready. We went with them to her brother-in-law's house and spent the night.

For the whole night, I could not sleep because of thinking about what could happen to us going out into the countryside. The only person who had insisted that we go was Juliana, my sister-in-law. Her family and her husband's relatives had not said anything. I prayed. Then something dawned on me. The Spirit nudged me, and I said, "No, I cannot go with them." In the morning, as Juliana loaded the truck, I told her, "I know you are doing this for me and my kids to go to a safe place, but, sorry, I cannot risk going with you guys." Then I walked with the kids about eight to ten miles back to my house. We had only three little bags to bring back.

The UNITA staff and the military personnel withdrew from the city into the bush during the nights. The majority of the people left the city running swiftly to the bush for safety. That night, a heavy rain came down for hours, and many people died fleeing the city, especially the small children. My children and I along with few other people stayed in the church basement for three days and nights. This church (Igreja dos Peregrinos) was less than a block away from my house. We could hear heavy shooting, bombs, and grenades falling outside the building during the days and the nights. I suppose I was strong since I had no other choice. At that time, even with people around me and my children, I felt so alone, and I longed for my husband. I spent those long nights and days praying and reading the Bible. I recall reading Isaiah 41:10 (NIV), "Do not fear, for I am your God. I will strengthen you and help you; I will uphold you with my righteous right hand."

After three days, the city seemed quiet. We went outside and saw the MPLA military cars on the streets with the soldiers telling us, "Be calm! Be calm! Be calm!" My children and I went back to our house. We saw some damages outside the house, but things inside were fine and intact. The following day, Ventura, my husband's relative, came to check on us. He brought food from his little grocery store in the suburbs. He was a very caring, compassionate, respectful, and nice person. He told me, "I take care of you and your children because your husband is the most highly remarkable and respectful person I have ever known."

From then on, there was much unrest. We heard of many who were arrested or killed. Then Ventura came back and asked me what else he could do for me. I asked him if he would take us to my parent's village about fifty miles away. I wanted the kids to be where there were no war activities, since nothing was happening yet in the remote villages. He replied, "Yes!" There were lots of military checkpoints along the road to my parents. But Ventura was ready for them because he had two identification cards (MPLA and UNITA). When he approached MPLA guards, he showed that party card and the other party card when needed for UNITA guards. Though I was comfortable to leave my kids with my parents, it was hard to be separated from them for the first time. Azevedo, the second son, was very attached to me. As we were leaving the house, he cried inconsolably and came running behind the car. My dad tried to go after him, but he could not catch him. Ventura stopped the car. We went back to the house walking with him. After promising to bring to him very special treats, he calmed down and was willing to stay.

> I take care of you and your children because your husband is the most highly remarkable and respectful person, I have ever known. (Ventura)

When I came back home without my kids, I resumed work as a nurse at the Central Hospital. The patients did not receive adequate care or enough medication. Sometimes, there were not enough beds. Sporadically, there were blackouts and no running water. Many workers were in danger because of the MPLA troops exchanging fire with the FNLA (another faction) troops in the city. Sometimes, the government soldiers went house to house searching. One day, they came to my house and searched everywhere. I think they were looking for hidden weapons. They did not find anything but tried to intimidate me. They confiscated my good camera sent by my husband a few weeks earlier. They gave excuses that they were preventing me from taking pictures of long lines at the grocery stores or of weapons used in Angola. They said that as a spy I could secretly send the film negatives overseas.

While the kids were at my parents, one day, they went to my parents' garden and uprooted some vegetable plants. My dad was upset and decided to punish or scare them. He called the children to him after inserting the whip in his belt behind him. The whip was a long stick with a flexible animal skin at the other end. As he was walking toward them, the kids noticed something sticking out from the top of his head. It was the whip. They were intimidated and ran away giggling. The situation was very bad because they all depended on those food products. Anibal, Azevedo, and Cicero vividly remember that experience up to now (2020).

After three months, the situation appeared somewhat calm in the city. I decided to bring my kids home from my parents. I had missed them so much and felt lonely without them. I talked to "brother" Ventura to see if he could take me to bring them home. He accepted my request, and we completed the round trip without incident. The children were very happy to see me, and they were eager to come back home.

Larry Henderson, Kye's husband, the former missionary in Angola, came to visit Nova Lisboa (Huambo) from the USA and took a picture of my children and me. He told me to write a short message to my husband in the United States. Briefly, I wrote a few lines in Umbundu and in Portuguese to let Joe know that the children and I were fine. Unfortunately, I could not write much, because of always being so apprehensive. Later, after observing so many things happening, I wrote to Joe, in the Umbundu language, "Life is getting very tough and dangerous."

Every day working at the hospital, I saw wounded people with serious injuries and unstable conditions brought in for treatment. I also saw dead people taken to the mortuary just a few yards away from the hospital. Many dead people were piled high, like sardines, in the mortuary. It was a nightmare to walk past it because of the smell! Later in the United States, when I watched the movie of the Ruanda massacre, I was reminded of Angola's tragedies. I could not finish watching that movie, because the Angolan dead people were continuously coming to my mind. When I wrote to my husband, one time I said to him, "If you don't see any more letters from me, that's it." We just took one day at a time. Fortunately, God was always our refuge and on our side. Again, I remembered the scriptures from Psalm 46:1 (NIV): "God is our refuge and strength, an ever-present help in trouble."

> If you don't see any more letters from me, that's it.

We heard of people being imprisoned or killed. Joe's cousin was arrested and taken to prison. We never heard from him again. One of Joe's closest friends was also taken to a prison and tortured, but he survived and came back to his family years later.

Do I Still Have a Family?

Not knowing whether our families were alive was crucial to the daily living of me and of the other students who had left their families in Angola. This was certainly a low point in my life. I was living in darkness and agony from October 1975 until May 1976 when Larry Henderson came back from visiting Angola. Larry brought us a couple of pictures and brief letters from our families. (See picture in the middle of the book.) Ana had not written much, because of fears of being punished since the government was censuring all written information. It was a great relief knowing that our families were okay. This ended the eight agonizing months without news from them. We sang alleluia to the Lord! We celebrated and praised God for His protection. However, my heart was very sad reading her letter of helplessness.

Some of us started thinking about the possibility of bringing the families to the United States. The Isaias (Anacleto), the Cornelio (Aarao), and the Chongola (Moises) families already had Portuguese passports before leaving Angola. They had been in Luanda, the capital city, either living or visiting. The families with passports could more easily travel overseas. Within a year or two, these families were able to come to the United States, joining their husbands as the families of students. Unfortunately, not foreseeing the future, I had left Ana without any traveling documents to leave Angola. Actually, no one realized how severe the civil war in Angola would become. I thought I could just return to my family upon graduation.

However, I always prayed and pleaded to God to protect my family and show me ways and open the doors for my family to get out of Angola. To further complicate the situation, I learned that young boys in Angola of ages seven years or older were being sent to Cuba to be taught how to handle guns. This increased my worries since two of my sons were ages eight and ten. I thought, *My family needs to get out.*

My Asking for Help, 1977

In Muncie, Indiana, I sang in both Eden United Church of Christ (now Eden Church) and Community United Church of Christ choirs where Don Orander and Fred Dare were pastors, respectively.

One Sunday in early 1977, after worshiping at the Community UCC, Fred and Nancy Dare invited me for lunch, as usual. I was physically well-fed, but my mind was still hungry and very disturbed. During the previous night, I had fervently prayed several times to ask for God's wisdom. After lunch, I asked Fred if we could have a private talk. He said, "Let's go to my office." My heart pumped quickly, thinking about what I would say to him. I was very apprehensive. We sat down and Fred, as usual, smiled at me, and said, "Jose, what do you have in mind?" With a big sigh, I briefly explained the escalation of the Angolan civil war and how it could physically impact my wife and children. At the end of my explanation, I asked him, "Would you pray and ask the congregation to pray with me?" Then I continued, "Is there any way that you could help me find a way to get my family out of Angola to the United States?" Without hesitation, Fred was compelled to reply, "We will find the way!" He continued, "In the past, we sponsored one Vietnamese family in our church, so I don't think this would be a problem for our congregation to sponsor another family." Then he said, "However, you should tell your wife to find a way to get out and go to a country where you can easily communicate."

> Would you pray and ask the congregation to pray with me? Is there any way that you could help me find a way to get my family out of Angola to the United States?

> We will find the way! (Fred)

Wow, I was speechless. "We will find the way! We will find the way!" I did not know what to do or how to start. I continuously prayed to God to intervene. God's presence is everywhere. I recalled Psalm 139:7–10 (NIV) as my consolation:

> Where I can go from your Spirit?
> Where can I flee from your presence?
> If I go up to the heavens, you are there;
> If I make my bed in depths, you are there.
> If I rise on the wings of the dawn,
> I settle on the far side of the sea,
> Even there your hand will guide me,
> Your right hand will hold me fast.

The Spirit of God interceded in Ana's thoughts and mine. Without anyone telling Ana, the Spirit told her to prepare to travel to Portugal. "We do not know what we ought to pray for, but the Spirit himself intercedes for us with groans that words cannot express" (1 Corinthians 8:26 NIV).

The Reunification Efforts Hit Barriers

On February 8, 1977, my sponsor, the African American Institute, sent a sponsor's statement to be completed by my family's sponsor. However, some issues were raised as to whether Ana could leave Angola for Portugal like other families. Also I received a letter from Mrs. Henderson, the institute's secretary, advising me to prepare for the family traveling to Portugal and to be ready to adjust to a new life of simultaneously being a student and supporting the family.

Fred Dare contacted the congregation and the members agreed to sponsor my family. The church filled out the statement of sponsorship signed by Pastor Dare and notarized by a church leader on April 26, 1977.

It was impossible to contact and advise Ana. However, I thought of a possible way to aid the process of getting the family from Angola.

In February 1977, I wrote a letter to Congressman Phil Sharp, tenth district of Indiana. He replied,

> February 22, 1977, Mr. Chimbanda:
> Thank you for contacting me regarding your desire to bring your family to the United States from Angola.
> I certainly, understand your concern in this matter, and I would like to be of all possible assistance to you. A member of my staff has contacted the Department of State on your behalf, expressing my interest and requesting information for you.
> I will be in touch with you as soon as such information is made available.
> Sincerely, signed Phil Sharp, Member of Congress

On March 28, 1977, the Department of State replied,

> Dear Congressman Sharp:
> Thank you for your inquiry of February 22, 1977 regarding Jose Chimbanda, an Angola student who wishes to bring his wife and children to the United States.
> We have asked the African-American Institute (AAI) to give us background information to use in responding to you. AAI is the contractor responsible for the implementation of the Development Training project in which Mr. Chimbanda is a participant.
> We will be back in touch with you as soon as we have a report from AAI.
> Sincerely yours, signed Jean P Lewis, Acting Assistant Administrator for Legislation Affairs

On April 25, 1977, Congressman Sharp replied with the follow-up information from the Department of State,

> Dear Mr. Chimbanda:
> This letter concerns your desire to bring your family to the United States.
> My office has been contacted by a representative of Department of State with the information that the Department cannot assist your family in moving from Angola. While the Department may help your family if they file a visa petition at the nearest American embassy, the actual move must be made without assistance from this country.
> I truly regret that the result of this inquiry could not be more favorable for you, Mr. Chimbanda.
> Sincerely, signed Phil Sharp, Member of Congress

There was nothing else I could do at this point except to pray to God that there would be someone traveling to Angola to suggest that Ana and the children leave our country as soon as possible. We could not communicate directly, but the Spirit was our liaison.

In June 1977, I was invited by Canadian missionaries to attend their annual meeting in Toronto. This regarded selection of Angolan high school graduates to receive Angola Memorial Scholarships. Also my intention was to seek help by telling the missionaries that my family was stranded in Angola. (Although I was just a member at large at this scholarship selection meeting, I was later granted two $1,000 scholarships for graduate school tuition.) After the meeting, I went to Mississauga Canada to help pack clothing to be shipped to the Angolan Congregational and Evangelical Churches for those in need. (See pictures at the end of the book.)

Ana Recalls More of Her Experiences in Angola

In March 1977, I flew about one hour to Luanda to start handling the travel documents. I was told I could get them in Nova Lisboa (Huambo). I went back there and tried, but to no avail. The only place I could get the documents was in Luanda. No one was giving me accurate information. There were many people trying to leave Angola for Portugal. After a couple of months, I again asked permission at my job to go to Luanda for a couple of weeks. I was told that the documents would take a month or more to process and that I would need my kids with me. Therefore, I went back to Nova Lisboa (Huambo) and requested medical leave to go to Portugal allegedly for an eye doctor visit.

In October, we flew to Luanda. I was able to communicate with Joe via people who were going in and out of Angola. This information was very limited to prevent suspicions. Still, Joe soon knew I was securing the paperwork to go to Portugal.

While in Luanda, my children and I stayed with our good friends, Tito Cornelio, MD, and Catarina Cassungo. We called them in Portuguese "*afilhados*," which means Joe and I were godparents in their wedding. They lived in an apartment which was too small to accommodate two families. My children and I moved in with Joe's cousin, Mariana Mandele, who lived with her family in a shack at outskirts of the city. This place was also not sufficient for two families. It had only two bedrooms. My kids and I slept in one bedroom and the other family in the other. The conditions were very precarious. There was no access to safe sanitation. The toilet was a small outdoor pit which served other residents too. No one was responsible for cleaning and using it properly. There were flies everywhere and worms around the pit. Only God was protecting us from diseases. It was amazing that none of us got sick.

Being too far from downtown, I asked our *afilhados* to allow us to come back to their apartment for just for a few days. I spent all the money I had brought with me. I still needed 1,000 *escudos* (Portuguese currency) more to complete the required documentation. This was about $100 in U S dollars. Tito gave me the money without hesitation. I was very appreciative and thankful for his generosity.

When we returned home, I continued efforts to leave Angola for Portugal. I got the rest of our savings and my last pay from work. Finally, in December of 1977, my kids and I got our travelling documents and tickets to fly to Portugal. I had to show a doctor's prescription, as if I were going to have my eyes checked in Portugal. I had to make it appear that we would be returning, so I purchased six expensive round-trip tickets. I had no other choice but to abandon most of our worldly possessions. I just needed to get my family out of Angola.

My Family Leaving Angola for Portugal

> Faith is being sure of what we hope for and certain of what we do not see. (Hebrews 11:1 NIV)

In December 1977, Ana and our five children—Anibal (eleven), Azevedo (nine), Cicero (seven), Arlindo (five), and Clarisse (three)—had permission to leave Angola and go to Portugal supposedly for Ana to see an eye doctor. Once in the plane, Ana was overjoyed in that it seemed the light was finally visible at the end of the tunnel. She was so happy to be leaving the deplorable conditions in her native country. On the other hand, she was scared of not knowing Portugal or anybody there except Alice Moreira. She was taking our young family into an unknown territory.

Joe had contacted Alice Moreira, who had worked as a missionary at Leprosarium mission station in Angola. Now living in Portugal, she was far from the airport in Lisbon. A few weeks before Ana and the children were scheduled to fly from Angola to Lisbon, Portugal, Alice had provided the name and address of the motel where they could stay in Portugal.

Ana was apprehensive boarding the airplane like Abraham was when he did not know where he was going. But Ana had the same faith as Abraham. "By faith Abraham, when called to go to a place he would later receive as his inheritance, obeyed and went, even though he did not know where he was going" (Hebrews 11:8 NIV). Ana recalled and believed in the words spoken to Moses: "Be strong and courageous. Do not be afraid or terrified…for the Lord your God goes with you; he will never leave you; nor forsake you" (Deuteronomy 31:6 NIV).

As Ana sat in the airplane, a nun was close to her. The nun wondered about the lady alone and very preoccupied and anxious with five young children. She asked Ana, "Where are you going?"

"To Lisbon."

"Do you have anybody waiting for you?"

"No."

"Do you have an address where you are going?"

"Yes."

"I will help you when we get there."

"Thank you."

Wow, what a Godsend! When they landed, the nun called a taxi, gave the driver the motel address, paid him, and gave him instructions to tell the receptionist at the motel to call her to reassure that the family had arrived there all right. Ana and the children got to the motel and checked in. The taxi driver gave the nun's phone number to the receptionist. This was the story of the Good Samaritan. Luke 10:25–37. Ana thought, "This nun was an angel appearing to me!" What a relief for the family to be out of the very dangerous Angola. It was difficult to leave home and almost all of our material possessions, but it was necessary. Basically, they had only "the clothes on their backs."

Alice Moreira called Fred Dare telling him the family had arrived in Portugal. Joe could now call Ana to talk with her and the children. (See pictures in the middle of the book.) Ana found out later that the motel (Pensao Madeira) was run by a family that had relocated from Angola.

Arranging for My Family to Arrive, 1978

After I heard the good news and talked to Ana and the children, I made arrangements to accommodate them with me. I moved from the dormitory to a university family housing apartment with two bedrooms. People from the UCC churches, Eden and Community, donated furniture, including two bunk beds and other basic supplies for the apartment. I made all the beds and saw that everything was ready for my family. I contacted the university regarding the School of Continuing Education's Basic English course.

I was joyfully anticipating the arrival of my family, after not seeing them for over two years. I had missed them dearly and feared terribly for their safety. There were so many new things to show them. I could hardly wait having no hint of more delays.

My Family Stranded in Portugal

We Face New Challenges

Just few days after they arrived in Portugal, Ana went confidently to the American embassy in Lisbon to secure their visas to the United States. Unfortunately, her enthusiasm was crushed. The embassy personnel denied the visas because Ana and the children did not have Angolan passports. Thus, they could not join me, a student with only a student visa in the United States. Ana called me crying on the phone. I knew something devastating had happened. She said, "The visas were denied." The lack of passports that have been a problem leaving Angola was now preventing them from leaving Portugal.

When I learned the bad news, I sunk in silence and shock. It was like a bomb falling on my body. What had seemed to be a high point was suddenly very low. For a few hours, I lived in a dim shadow of the world, and I did not understand why. My heart was as gloomy as the overcast skies outside. I explained the bad news to Pastor Dare. He was also stunned. Our high hopes were destroyed, but our faith was still strong. We realized that our work must continue. Obviously, we had more hardships to endure.

Still busy with my school assignments, I agonized about what to do. I went to the library to study, but my energies were divided. About half of my time, I concentrated on studies, and the other half, I used to try to determine how to get my family to America. In the meantime, I continued to put my faith in God, have patience, and get lots of strength inside me. I dwelled on the scriptures in Philippians 4:13 (NIV), "I can do everything through him who gives me strength." I shared this verse with Ana. We realized that we could no longer dictate our actions but things had to be handled by our Almighty God.

> In the meantime, I continued to put my faith in God, have patience, and get lots of strength inside me.

> God provides food for the birds, but does not put it in their nests. (Harold Brown)

I have heard the phrase "God provides food for the birds, but does not put it in their nests." James 2:26 strongly wrote that "faith without works is dead." We maintained our faith but understood that we must also work toward accomplishing our goals. One of the monks used a Latin phrase "ora et labora," meaning "pray and work."

> Ora et labora. (Pray and work). (Latin phrase)

Thus, we continued and increased our efforts. On March 28, 1978, I sent a letter to the prime minister, Dr. Mario Soares, in Portugal to seek help for issuing Ana and the children Portuguese passports. I feared that this was not possible, but there was always the hope of a miracle. Eventually, this request was denied. Meanwhile, Ana even took our children with her to beg for visas, but they said, "Lady, no!"

On May 22, 1978, the Muncie Press published in the *Muncie Evening Press* an article of my interview with an editor, entitled, "Wife, Children in Portugal—BSU Angolan seeks Reunion with family" (not pictured in the book).

> Wife, Children in Portugal—BSU Angolan seeks Reunion with family. (The Muncie Press)

Suspension of My Scholarship

On June 5, 1978, I got a letter from the African American Institute stating,

> Dear Mr. Chimbanda:
>
> We have today sent you the following mailgram:
>
> "Deeply regret to inform you that your scholarship is placed in grave jeopardy due to AID's interpretation of Congressional Foreign Assistance Act. No program funding available for your continued support effective immediately. AAI continuing efforts to secure reconsideration of this action while exploring alternate means of support. Call your AAI Program Officer for more details. Letter follows.' The Development Training Program for Portuguese-Speaking Africa (DTPSA), under which you are presently studying, is financed, as you know, by the United States Agency for International Development (AID), which in turns receives its funds through annual appropriations of the United States Congress. Normally, funds would be available to support all participants in good standing through the completion of their approved study programs. However, in May of this year, we were informed by AID of '...prohibitions on the use of AID funds to finance training of Angolan participants under our contract with the institute...' We were informed that this prohibition came out of the fact that Congressional Action has limited the use of AID funds to finance any assistance to Angola. The Letter from AID stated that: '...Section 114 of the FY 1978 appropriation bill provides: 'None of the funds appropri-

ated or made available pursuant to this Act shall be obligated or expended to finance directly any assistance to Mozambique or Angola.' This legislation has been interpreted to prohibit financing of Angolans under the regional project...

In view of the circumstances, you will immediately terminate the use of AID funds for the training of the 24 Angolans currently in the United States, the two Angolan participants who are training in Tunisia and the nine Angolans awaiting training in Africa.'

We deeply regret that this situation has arisen and wish to express to you our fullest concern about the extremely distressing position in which we are all placed by this action. We have continued to protest to AID and the Department of State, and to work with the members of Congress in an effort to secure a reconsideration or modification of this action which would permit us to continue your support. Unless there is a reversal of the AID decision, we will not have the means to provide you with any additional support. We are aware that you will be alarmed by this news. We wish to assure you that we are doing, and will continue to do, everything possible to find a solution to this problem. We are hopeful that even if the 1978 fiscal year restrictions are not removed, that similar restrictions will not be imposed on the FY 1979 funds to be appropriated by Congress. Such funds would become available as of October 1, 1978. If the FY 1978 restrictions are not again imposed, we would then hope to be able to resume your support in October. This possibility about the 1979 fiscal year funds still leaves you to confront the difficult prospect of a 3-month period without our financial support. By copy of this letter, we are also informing the Foreign Student Advisor at your Institution of this new development. We suggest that you discuss other options with him such as the possibility of securing summer employment or of obtaining some assistance from local groups in your community. Please keep us informed of any prospects that may develop for you. We are again express our profound concern that this situation has arisen. We shall exert every effort to get a reversal of his decision and shall continue to keep you informed of all future developments regarding this problem."

This long letter was signed by Wilbur Jones, director of Education. It brought more very bad news at an already overwhelming time. My valuable scholarship was suspended. This aggravated me greatly battling one crisis after another. I took summer school off and found work on campus. I cleaned and painted the family housing apartments. The physical labor allowed my mind some temporary relief from my worries.

Unfortunately, on June 30, I got a letter from the African American Institute informing that they were unable to secure a reversal of the scholarship termination. However, they did provide a small amount of emergency money to cover room and board. So my scholarship was definitely gone.

God always provides like when Abraham was willing to sacrifice his only son, God provided a ram to sacrifice instead of his son. Genesis 22:13–14 (NIV) says, "Abraham looked up and there in a thicket he saw a ram caught by its horns… So Abraham called that place the Lord Will Provide." I secured a loan to cover the tuition and continued my studies and life alone.

Pastor Dare continued working by making many contacts. (I learned later that he had made a folder named "Immigration," containing ten handwritten pages with names and phone numbers, addresses, and notes. He was meticulous and definitely took my problems seriously.) His efforts would eventually help us.

> For better or worse, richer or poorer, in
> sickness or health.

I remember the vows that Ana and I made at our religious wedding: "For better or worse, richer or poorer, in sickness or health." Nothing should ever separate our family. Judges 11:35 (NIV) says, "I have made a vow to the Lord that I cannot break." Also the biblical scriptures say, "Ask and it will be given to you; seek and you will find; knock and the door will be opened to. For everyone who asks receives; he who seeks finds, and to him who knocks, the door will be opened" (Matthew 7:7–8 NIV). We stood relentlessly firm, and nothing moved us backward. Surely good news would come.

Help from Churches and the Church World Service

After a month, my family did not have money to survive in Portugal. I did not have enough to send them any support. I continued praying, crying on my knees to God, fasting, and making contacts.

Fred Dare relentlessly wrote letters to anyone he thought would help. He made contacts with other UCC churches around the Muncie area to solicit financial support. He opened a bank account, "the Chimbandas Fund," where the churches could make deposits. The money was periodically sent to Ana. At some point, Ana's travel documents to go back to Angola expired. Definitely, she was illegally stranded in Portugal with no other country where she could go legally.

The Church World Service's Immigration & Refugee Program provided a grant of $350 per month for two months or until the possible success of reuniting the family. This was an agreement between that office and Ms. Joyce Myers, the former American missionary in Angola. They were corresponding with Pastor Dare. They also sent letters of encouragement to me. A few months later, the Church

World Services sent a check of $1,000 to Ana. We later learned that those funds had been raised by the CROP Hunger Walk. This was why we have been passionate and very active in the CROP Hunger Walk up to the present time 2020. The value of that $1,000 was more than just monetary.

My Family Predicaments

The red tape was extensive and binding. The predicaments were (1) with just a student visa, I could not stay in the United States after graduation; (2) having no passports, Ana and our family could not legally stay in Portugal or return to Angola; (3) also without passports, Ana and the children could not go to any country; (4) having been treasurer of UNITA, I could not return safely to Angola. UNITA was losing the civil war, and many of my relatives had been persecuted and some had been killed; (5) after graduation, I could go to Portugal to visit my family; and (6) I could visit Portugal but not become a legal resident, because I did not have a Portuguese passport. My only passport had been issued by the Angolan interim government which no longer existed. In summary, our family was separated without any legal ways to reunite.

Suggestions and More Attempts

I was informed by Ms. Alice Moreira that one of the leaders of UNITA suggested that Ana and the children should be sent to Zaire where the American embassy had good relations with UNITA. I disagreed with the suggestion because of the dismal failure with the American embassy in Lisbon, Portugal.

It was suggested that I write letters to senators and congressmen to plead our case. I sent twenty letters, including to Senator Birch Bayh Sr. of Indiana and Senator Edward Kennedy of Massachusetts.

Fred Dare made an appointment with Congressman Phil Sharp in Muncie. Along with several friends, we met with the congressman to present my case. The supporters were Norma Carmichael, Charlene Suldovsky, Winiford Bryant, Beth Hall, Nancy Dare,

Sharon Brown, Rosie Wells, and Billie Kennedy. We had a good discussion, but I don't remember any tangible benefit of the meeting.

Fred and I made a trip to Washington, DC. We were very hopeful of finding a way to have my family permitted to join me. We were there for two days visiting the Portuguese embassy and the offices of Phil Sharp and Senator Birch Bayh. We invested considerable time, energy, and money but were disappointed that no success was evident. (See pictures in the middle of the book.)

We spent the night at the apartment of Marcos Samondo (now deceased). He had been my English language classmate. The apartment had some cockroaches of which we joked by saying we had other roommates in the apartment. Marcos had a strong sense of humor. We enjoyed having fun with Marcos. It was a welcome relief.

In April 1979, Fred Dare made a second trip to Washington, DC, to follow some leads. The mother of an important lawyer had updated her son on our situation. (This attorney was working for the secretary of state and had been a general counsel at the State Department during the President Gerald Ford administration.) After meeting with the interested attorney, Fred went to the UCC legislative headquarters across the street from the Supreme Court and to Congressman Phil Sharp's office. While there, he called the undersecretary of state and made an appointment. However, the scheduled meeting had been canceled when Fred arrived for it. Someone suggested that Fred call a well-known attorney who was a friend of the UCC and was very influential with immigration. After Fred explained everything, the well-known attorney called the undersecretary who confirmed that the meeting had been canceled and that nothing could be done.

The attorney decided to set up a press conference with one of the attorneys. Fred acknowledged Congressman Sharp and invited his assistant to go with Fred to the meeting. They did not only meet that attorney but also the head of the Visa Department plus an official of the Justice Department. Fred presented our case and suggested that they grant political asylum quickly as they had done for others. They said, "Reverend, you would not want us to break the law, would you?" Fred retorted, "No, I would not want you to break the law but to interpret the law and decide on it." After more discussion, they suggested that I request asylum. If this were approved, they would grant my family permission to join me for humanitarian reasons. This was not just a ray of hope but a miracle made possible by the dedication and persistence of Reverend Dare! (His chance meeting with my Illinois pastor had been amazingly fortunate for us.)

Afterward, Fred went to the United Nations in New York to see the high commissioner for the Immigration and Refugees, but nothing happened. Moreover, Fred contacted the Indianapolis News Station (Channel 13) to follow up the story to seek support and help.

Ana Recalls Her Life in Portugal, 1978

We settled in the Pensao Madeira Motel. We were praying daily that the American embassy in Lisbon, Portugal, would give us visas to permit our trip to the United States. Unfortunately, the situation remained very complicated because we did not have the needed legal documents. My children and I were waiting at the door of the US embassy almost every morning. Eventually, the guard allowed us to go inside, but nothing was approved. Then Alice Moreira came to support us, and we both tried to explain my hope of joining my husband. The embassy denied all our requests. We stayed at Pensao for a few more weeks but could not afford to stay any longer.

There was a lady, Maria Jose de Oliveira, living in Costa de Caparica, in the suburb of Lisbon. She had been my teacher in Angola, when I was studying in the mission station of Dondi. She still remembered my name among the many students she had taught. She and her husband graciously asked us to live with them in their house. She was married to Jorge and had three girls, close to the ages of my older children. Their house had two bedrooms, a small kitchen, a family room, and one bathroom. Each family used a bedroom with their children. It was truly a sacrifice for them to host us. It eventually took away all their privacy. Jorge was an excellent, compassionate, and caring person. He treated my children as if they were his own. Occasionally, he took all eight children to the beach to play. After lunch, Jorge showed a Brazilian television soap opera

Escrava Isaura for all to watch. (The Portuguese took two hours off for lunch, and normally, the employees went home to eat and rest.)

One morning, Anibal and I decided to go to another suburb of Lisbon to meet with Mr. Pinto Ribeiro, who had been the pastor of our church of Peregrinos in Huambo, Angola. It was necessary to cross the River Tejo with fees to ride the boat. Mr. Ribeiro had a son who lived in Canada. Trying all the possible means to get to United States, I thought Mr. Ribeiro could possibly make some connections with his son to arrange for us to go through Canada. Unfortunately, it did not work. Coming back disappointed and as we approached the house, we saw lots of commotion. When Maria Jose saw me from a distance, she ran and hugged me, saying, "Aah, Jorge is dead!" (Ai [*eye*], Jorge morreu!" Oh my, what a shock! We hugged and cried bitterly. Jorge, as usual, had been watching the television with the kids at lunchtime. The kids saw Jorge collapsing and called his wife. They tried CPR and everything possible to save his life, but to no avail. He had died of a heart attack.

Maria Jose, now a widow, without a financial supporter decided to rent one of her rooms to earn a little income. Therefore, she asked me to find another place to live. Life was not easy for me and for my kids. I remembered Romans 5:3–5 (NIV): "That suffering produces perseverance; perseverance, character; character, hope; and hope does not disappoint us…" I called Ms. Alice Moreira, who suggested that we go back to the Pensao Madeira Motel.

The motel had got worse and was overcrowded with many more refugees from Angola and Mozambique. I had a small room with a bed and a small electric stove. To sleep, I had two kids on each side of the bed and another at the foot. Six families shared an outside bathroom. For us to have our bathroom turn, I had to go with the kids at 5:00 a.m. Then between 6:30 a.m. and 7:00 a.m., I started work at the motel. I washed the linens and helped with the kitchen chores. My oldest son, Anibal, took care of his siblings.

Since the time was flying by without any success, I decided to enroll the three oldest sons in school. After school, Anibal sold the sports newspaper on the street to earn some money. We went to a Baptist Church close to the motel. The church members were very encouraging and compassionate. At nights, after the kids went to bed, I spent time reading the Bible and praying. (See picture in the middle of the book.)

One Sunday afternoon, there was a special children's program at the church. Unfortunately, I did not take them, because I needed to do some housework while they were gone. I let them go by themselves. I instructed them to always walk together by holding hands especially when crossing the street. At the street intersection, Arlindo, our youngest boy, broke away from the hand chain to run across the street alone. A taxicab hit him. Fortunately, he was not severely injured, but he was terrified. Anibal told his brother Azevedo to run home and tell me. Azevedo ran home excitedly and swiftly, accidently bumping into an electricity pole. He came to my room crying and, without any real explanation, said, "Mom, come. Please come, Arlindo!" I said, "Azevedo, what is wrong with you and Arlindo?" His forehead was bleeding slightly. We immediately ran to the location and found that Arlindo had already been taken by ambulance to the local hospital. Azevedo and I took a taxicab to the emergency section and ran inside. We found Arlindo holding his arm, fearfully saying, "Mom, please don't cry. I am okay." My situation was so critical that even the kids avoided telling me anything that would add an extra burden on me. Apparently, they saw me crying occasionally.

Arlindo's arm was clearly broken, and he had some scratches on his forehead. The X-rays showed two broken bones (ulna and radius). (See picture in the middle of the book.) They put a cast on him and hospitalized him for five days. They also treated Azevedo's scratches.

We thanked God that the hospital treatment in Portugal was free. I had to deal only with him getting well rather than also with the bills. Our church played a big role in my life at this time of need. The members of the church helped me with visitation, transportation, and prayers. It reminded me of how important it is to belong to a church organization wherever you are.

Activities, Some Responses, and a Ray of Hope, 1979

At the end of 1978, without any apparent success, Alice Moreira wrote to Church World Service reporting that four Chimbanda children were in school, by the kindness of the United Nations. She requested to extend the financial help for 1979 since there was still no progress.

On March 2, 1979, Senator Kennedy replied,

> Dear Mr. Chimbanda: Thank you very much for your recent letter. It has been a long tradition and Congregational courtesy to refer correspondence from another state to one of the Senator from that state. This gives each member of Congress the opportunity to be of service to the constituents they directly serve. For this reason, I am sure you understand why I am forwarding your correspondence to Senator Bayh from your state. Adding my hope that the matter can be resolved to your satisfaction as soon as possible. Again, I appreciate your taking the time to contact me. Sincerely, Signed Edward M Kennedy.

On March 3, 1979, Senator Bayh replied,

> Dear Mr. Chimbanda: Thank you for your recent correspondence. I am pleased that you asked for my help and have contacted the Department of State in your behalf. As soon as a response is received, I will contact you again. Again, thank you for this opportunity to assist you. With best regards, I remain Sincerely, Signed Birch Bayh.

On April 8, 1979, Senator Bayh forwarded me a response copy from the Department of State's response to his inquiry on my behalf:

April 3, 1979, Dear Senator Bayh, I refer to your letter of March 5 concerning the desire of Mr. Jose Chimbanda to be granted asylum in the United States and to have his family join him here.

Since the Immigration and Naturalization Service (INS) has jurisdiction over aliens in the United States, decisions regarding asylum rest with that Service. Doubtful cases or cases considered to be lacking in merit a referred to us by the INS for review. Our views are then considered by the Service when making a decision on such a request for asylum.

Regarding Mr. Chimbanda's request, it is our view that he has established a well-founded fear of persecution upon return to Angola. However, it was noted that he entered the United States on a Portuguese passport. The United States Supreme Court held in the Rosenburg vs Yee Chien Woo 402 U.S. 49 (1971) that an alien who asserts a claim to refugee status must establish that his presence in the United States is a consequence of his flight in search of refuge. The physical presence must be one which is reasonably proximate to the flight and not one following a flight remote in point of time or intervening residence in a third country reasonably constituting a termination of the original flight in search of refuge. The question of intervening residence in a third country, or of "firm resettlement," is largely a factual question which, once that fact appears of record, the applicant has the burden of overcoming (Chinese American Civic

Council v. Attorney General of the United States, 566 F. 2d 321, 1977.

Article 1 of the United Nations Convention Relating to the Status of Refugees addresses the situation in which a refugee possesses more than one nationality: "In the case of a person who has more than one nationality, the term 'the country of his nationality' shall mean each of the countries of which he is a national, and a person shall not be deemed to be lacking the protection of the country of his nationality if, without an valid reason based on well-founded fear (of being persecuted), he has not availed himself of the protection of one of the countries of which he is a national." The issuance of Portuguese passport to Mr. Chimbanda is a matter of record and implies that he was considered a national of Portugal at the time of its issuance and that he voluntarily availed himself of the protection of Portugal. Under the circumstances, it is our view that Mr. Chimbanda must document to the satisfaction of the INS his inability to return to Portugal.

If the INS believes that his inability to obtain a Portuguese residence visa sufficiently documents his inadmissibility to Portugal and, therefore, allows him to remain in this country as a refugee, the Department would support a request by Mr. Chimbanda to the Immigration Service to allow his family's admission into this country for family reunification.

Wow, this information provided a ray of hope. A possible solution was for me to go to a Portuguese embassy and secure a letter denying me permission to enter Portugal. Then I could be considered a person without a country. Therefore, based on humanitarian needs, the United States could accept me as a refugee and probably allow my family to join me. I drove to the Portuguese embassy in Chicago to explain my case. I was advised to write a letter explaining what was needed. I gladly wrote the letter. In a few weeks, I got the much-anticipated letter from the embassy stating denial of my being Portuguese. It seemed that the only remaining step involved action by the immigration people. I needed better luck for that to occur in anything close to a timely manner.

I forwarded the letter to the Immigration and Naturalization Service. After a few months of difficult waiting, I contacted them but was asked to resubmit the same letter. I had to send a copy of that same letter three or four times. The slow moving or no-moving bureaucracy of the Immigration and Naturalization Service delayed our reunification by four or five months. I shared with Ana. Romans 5:2b–5 (NIV) says, "Not only so, but we also we rejoice in our sufferings, because suffering produces perseverance; perseverance, character; character hope. And hope does not disappoint us, because God has poured out his love into our hearts by the Holy Spirit, whom he has given us." *Hope...*

The Miracle Sunday May, 1979

Some time later the brook dried up because there had been no rain in the land. Then the word of the Lord came to Elijah: "Go at once to Zarephath of Sidon and stay there. I have commanded a widow in that place to supply you with food." So he went... When he came to the town gate, a widow was there gathering sticks. He called to her and asked, "Would you bring me a little water in a jar so I may have a drink? As she was going to get it, he called, and bring me, please, a piece of bread"... She Replied, "I don't have any bread—only a handful of flour in a jar and a little oil in a jug. I am gathering a few sticks to take home and make a meal for myself and my son that we may eat it—and die." Elijah

said to her, "Don't be afraid. Go home and do as
you have said… The jar of flour will not be used
up and the jug of oil will not run dry until the
day of the Lord gives rain on the land." (1 King
17:7–16 NIV)

When our children were very young, we usually gave each a
coin for the church offering plates. Ana's parents and my parents had
done the same thing for us when we were little. The first seeds had
been planted in us, and we were just passing it on as a family tradition. Hebrews 13:7 (NIV) depicts, "Remember your leaders, those
who spoke the word of God to you; consider the outcome of their
way of life, and imitate their faith."

On Mother's Day, Sunday, in 1979, Ana and the children were
still in Portugal. During the offering, I had only twenty-five cents.
I thought without hesitation, *I will be fine even if I give this quarter.* After the main offering, Sharon Brown, the lady who was in the
charge of their outreach missions, stood up and announced, "I have
this ribbon taped with glue stickers. Please, after the worship, place
any bill you have on the tape." She took the taped ribbon from the
pulpit to the church exit. The Community Church attendance in
Muncie was usually eighty to one hundred people. The total money
collected from the ribbon was exactly $250. One of the ladies had
brought a card that all the ladies had signed. On the top of the card,
Sharon had written,

> Dear Ana, In America we have a special day
> each year when we honor our mothers. This year
> our thoughts are with you and so each of us has
> signed our names to let you know we care and
> pray for your family—The Mothers, Daughters
> and Guests of Community United Church of
> Christ—Mother Daughter Banquet 1979.

The card and a certified check for $250 were mailed to Ana
in Portugal. What a miracle! It seemed that my "twenty-five cents"

had been multiplied by one thousand. It was like Jesus feeding five thousand people with five loaves of bread and two fish. Matthew 14:13–21.

> It seemed that my "twenty-five cents" had
> been multiplied by one thousand.

Even today, our church offering has remained a number one priority. When Ana and I make our weekly budget, we write down on the monthly expense first our tithe offering to our church because God has given us too many blessings to count. We believe, "But seek first his kingdom and his righteousness, and all these things will be given to you as well" (Matthew 6:33 NIV).

Requests for My Family to Join Me

The Social Service Department of the Immigration and Refugee Program, under the Church World Service, sent me a draft letter and advised me to apply for political asylum in the United States and that the letter should be addressed to "Commissioner, Immigration and Naturalization Service, U. S. Department of Justice, Washington D.C."

On February 27, 1979, Elise Tsomaia, the Social Service supervisor of Immigration and Refugee Program, reminded Mr. Arthur of their telephone conversation with the following letter:

> Dear Mr. Arthur:
> Re: CHIMBANDA, Jose and Family
> As per our telephone conversation, please find enclosed the document from the Portuguese Consulate and the translation together with the letter of Mr. Jose CHIMBANDA.
> Will you please look into this case and let us know what chances Mr. CHIMBANDA has. As you know, Mr. Chimbanda has a wife and five children and this office is helping them to survive. It

is our deep concern to bring the family as soon as possible.

Should Mr. CHIMBANDA be recognized as a refugee—Principal applicant—his family in Portugal might be eligible to come to the United States, under the Parole program.

Your help and advice will be greatly appreciated. Sincerely, (Signed)
The Social Service Supervisor
Immigration and Refugee Program

In March 1979, the State Department Refugee and Migration officer of the Bureau of Human Rights and Humanitarian Affairs reviewed my documents and agreed on my inability to obtain a Portuguese residence visa, so Mr. Arthur forwarded my case to the United States Immigration and Naturalization Service.

Pastor Dare wrote an urgent letter to the Congregational Relations of the State Department to prod them to review our request quickly:

May 29, 1979
Mr. Douglas J. Bennet, Jr.
Assistant Secretary for
Congregational Relations
The State Department
Washington, D. C. 20520
Re: Jose Chimbanda
(I.N.S. number not listed)

Dear Mr. Bennet:

I wrote to you April 11, 1979 concerning the Problem of Mr. Chimbanda. To date we have received no reply, nor has there been any further word from I.N.S.

Again may we urge you to assist us in determining the status of Mr. Chimbanda's request for Asylum and reunification with his family.

We are at a loss to understand why our government representatives will not recognize the urgency and the desperate situation of Mrs. Chimbanda and her five Children; living in Lisbon, Portugal as refugees without any funds or support. We are further perplexed about this, as we are asked by our National Church Agencies to assist in sponsoring and resettling refugees at the request of the United States Government. We have indeed responded to that call by sponsoring two Vietnamese families, as did a number of our sister churches in this area. And now we've been asking constantly for one and one-half years to assist this family—which would alleviate their suffering—to no avail.

As citizens, we feel that our government is being unresponsive and insensitive to this very real human need. I have been told that there are thousands in the same situation, but I believe that we deal in one number at a time, and the problem of this number could be quickly resolved.

We urge once again your cooperation and response.

Sincerely,
Fred Dare

Copies to: Ms. Gretchen Eik, Mr. Klaus Feldman, Congregational Phil Sharp, Senator Birch Bayh, Ms. Nancy Nicalo

In response, the Immigration and Refugee Program of the Church World Service wrote,

June 25, 1979
Mr. John Rebsamen
Refugees and Parole
United States Department of Justice
Immigration and Naturalization Service
425 "I" Street, N.W.
Washington, D. C. 20536

Dear Mr. Rebsamen:

We present to you, material related to the request for humanitarian parole for the wife and children of Mr. Jose Chimbanda.

Mr. Chimbanda has now been granted asylum in the United States as a refugee from Angola, per attached letter from the Immigration and Naturalization Service in Chicago.

Further, we also enclose a copy of Mr. Chimbanda's letter to the Commissioner of the Immigration and Naturalization Service, in which he is requesting humanitarian parole for his Wife and the children.

We do trust that you will look with favor upon this request and we look forward to hearing from you.

Sincerely yours, Nancy L. Nicalo, Director
Refugee Program
Enc.

c.c. to Pastor Fred Dare, Mr. Jose Chimbanda

Approval That My Family May Join Me

In July, I got a copy of a letter from the Social Service supervisor of the Immigration and Refugee Program sent to the Associate Commissioner at the United States Department of Justice, Immigration and Naturalization Service, in Washington, DC, to show appreciation for allowing the parole of the wife and children of Mr. Chimbanda, as per his letter of July thirteenth. First letter:

> Immigration & Refugee Program
> Nancy L Nicalo, Director
> July 10, 1979
> Pastor Fred Dare
> Community United Church of Christ
> 5706 Aubrey Lane
> Muncie, Indiana 47303
>
> Dear Pastor Dare:
> Re: Chimbanda, Ana Isabel and Family
> Following my telephone conversation yesterday, this is to inform that Commissioner Castillo has authorized the parole of the family of Jose Chimbanda. We are very happy for this development.
> Thank you for all your determination and energy you have put into this. I know you have already informed Mr. Chimbanda.
> The American Embassy will be in touch with Mrs. Chimbanda. If there is anything we can do, please let us know.
> Sincerely yours. (signed) (Mrs.) Elise Tsomaia,
> Social Service Supervisor, Immigration and Refugee Program

The second letter:

> (Postmark) Jul 13, 1979
> Ms. Nancy L. Nicalo
> Director, Refugee Program
> Church World Service
> 475 Riverside Drive

New York, NY 10027

Dear Ms. Nicalo:

I am responding to your letter with enclosures from Mr. Jose Chimbanda who has been granted political asylum in the United States requesting that his wife and five children be paroled into the United States from Portugal.

Since the government of Portugal has denied Mr. Chimbanda's application to reside in Portugal with his family, all of whom entered Portugal from Angola, for humanitarian reasons and in the interest of family reunification parole has been approved in behalf of the family which assigned file numbers.

	Ana Isabel Catuta Chimbanda	1-16-47
1.	Anibal Graca Joao Chimbanda	10-3-66
2.	Azevedo Crisostomo Chimbanda	10-21-68
3.	Cicero Mario Chimbanda	3-31-70
4.	Arlindo Samuel Chimbanda	4-23-72
5.	Clarisse Joana Chimbanda	10-22-74

This Service requested the Office of Refugee and Migration Affairs, Department of State on July 6, 1979 to notify the American Embassy, Lisbon, Portugal to issue the family a transportation letter which will enable the airline to bring them to the United States without visas. The Consular officer has been notified that the parole is conditional upon obtaining appropriate security clearances for Mrs. Chimbanda and that the family is found otherwise admissible to the United States.

The letter concluded,

Sincerely, and was signed by Carl J. Wacker,
Jr. Associate Commission Examinations.

Wow, I could not believe it for a while after I read the two letters. I read them multiple times. It was official. Alleluia! My family
could join me in the United States because I had no other country where I could reside. Hence, I was being granted asylum in the
United States as a political refugee. This new status made it permissi-
ble for my family to join me on humanitarian parole. It ended almost
four years of uncertainty, fear, and emotional low points during our
family separation. It was unfathomable the way the things were handled. God and His people had worked behind the scenes!

I called my Ana in Lisbon. I called my friends to let them know
the great news! I was excited and at the same time praising the Lord
for what He had done. "Thanks be to God! He always gives us the
victory, through our Lord Jesus Christ" (1 Corinthians 15:57 NIV).
Then Pastor Dare and other members of the church bought the tickets electronically for my family.

Family Reuniting and Adjusting in the United States

Family Reunited on July 22, 1979

This is the day the Lord has made;

> Let us rejoice and be glad in it. (Psalm 118:24 NIV)

> A very large crowd spread their cloaks on the road, while others cut branches from the trees and spread them on the road. The crowds that went ahead of him that followed shouted, Hosanna… Blessed… Hosanna… "When Jesus entered Jerusalem, the whole city was stirred and asked, 'Who is this?'—(the people from remote locations, like Simon of Cyrene)—The crowds answered, 'This is Jesus, the prophet from Nazareth in Galilee.'" (Matthew 21:8–11 NIV)

The people were possibly the ones closest to Jesus or who had been healed or fed by Him. In any case, this passage reminds me of my family's reunification.

I had been counting down years, months, weeks, and now days and hours. Perhaps absence does make the heart grows fonder. I hardly slept that night. Maybe I was dreaming, I thought. I woke up in the morning, and I said (paraphrased from Psalm 118:24), "This is the day the Lord has made for me; let me rejoice and be glad in it, indeed!"

On July 22, 1979, at about 5:30 p.m., I rode to the Community United Church of Christ with my friends Manuel and Ann Mpinga. I wore a traditional Angolan outfit which was a red-and-blue shirt with ornamented gold seams, red stripes, and blue long and wide-open-seamed pants with high black-and-white shoes. My hair and beard were well groomed.

> This is the day the Lord has made for me; let me rejoice and be glad in it, indeed! (Paraphrased from Psalm 118:24; Jose)

At the church, my strongest supporter, Pastor Dare, loaded everyone on the bus. There were about forty members, plus my friends from Ball State University. Friends included Abigal from Ethiopia, David Thiger and Shadrack Ambiche from Kenya, and Maliki from the Ivory Coast. Thus, about fifty of us headed to the Indianapolis airport to welcome my family from Portugal.

Everyone wanted to help celebrate our family's reunification after almost four years of separation. What a joy I had in my heart that my dreams were finally coming true! We waited anxiously at the TWA gate. The WTHR-TV Indiana's News Channel 13 reporter followed up on a story by interviewing Pastor Dare and me. The reporter asked me, "What are you going to do when you meet your family?" I said, "I will embrace them. This is for sure!" At 9:00 p.m., the people held a banner, written in Portuguese, "Bem vindo (welcome) *Ana, Anibal, Azevedo, Cicero, Arlindo, and Clarisse*!" I had no idea that there were going to be things like that. Everyone was enthusiastic, singing songs of joy and victory, and clapping their hands. There were tears of joy and lots of laughing. A number of people came from other gates and joined ours similar to a crowd of people following Jesus on the Palm Sunday asking, "Who is coming on that airplane?" The people who knew me said, "The wife and the children of an African family who are coming from Portugal, reuniting with her husband and their father."

At 9:20 p.m., the plane from La Guardia airport in New York City landed! Standing with Roland Stillwagon, my Sunday School teacher, I was anxiously smiling and looking at the gate hallway. At 9:27, Arlindo, our youngest boy, showed up first wearing a brown suit. I lifted him up and said, "Bem vindo, meu filho!" (Welcome, my son!) At 9:28, Azevedo, our second son, appeared wearing a red jacket. Then Cicero, our third son, came in a blue-and-white-striped jacket. Then Anibal, our oldest son, came with a brown sweater and carry-on luggage. To each, I said, "Bem Vindo, meu filho." The last two were Ana in a long blue-and-white flowered dress covered by a brownish sweater, holding Clarisse, our youngest child, who was in a white-and-blueish-colored dress, carrying her little purse. Lifting my only daughter, I looked straight into her eyes as she shyly bent her neck and looked down at me with her eyes open wide. I said, "Bem Vindo! Saudades! Amo te!" (Welcome! Miss you! I love you!) At 9:30, Ana smiled and looked at me as I held Clarisse up and tight to my chest. Finally, after putting Clarisse down, I saw my Ana patiently waiting her turn (maybe thinking of a dream coming true). She came close to me, and with close eye contact, we hugged and kissed with tears and laughs, and I said, "A nossa batalha terminou!" (The fight is over!) She replied, "Certamente!" (Certainly!) This was certainly a life high point. (See pictures in the middle of the book.)

> A nossa batalha terminou! (The fight is over!) (Jose)

> Certamente! (Indeed!) (Ana)

We loaded the bus and headed toward Muncie. The people sang songs of joy with lots of laugher. A few miles before getting to the Community United Church of Christ, two fire trucks (arranged by someone in the congregation) went ahead of the bus with a loud siren leading us to the church. We went into the church building and down into the Fellowship Hall, where drinks and two big cakes of welcome were awaiting us. Ana cut her first cake in the United States! I put a piece of cake on the plate, and someone passed it on to another person. Ana cut the cakes, and I placed each piece on plates as we served all that had come to celebrate our family unity. Everyone mingled, celebrated, and ate the cake with the fruit punch until 1:30 a.m. It seemed that the excitement delayed everyone's fatigue.

Afterward, we were driven to our residence in the family housing apartments at Ball State University. (See picture in the middle of the book.) What a glorious day and night! All the praises went to Him! The next evening, TV Channel 13 aired their coverage of our big day and prior events. Friends who had not gone to the airport had an opportunity to see our family reunification.

With the help of many friends from the UCC Churches, I had gotten my family to the United States. God had worked miraculously in this process, and things were gradually unfolding for us after the years apart. It reminds us of the scripture "The secret things belong to the Lord our God, but the things revealed belong to us and to our sons forever" (Deuteronomy 29:29 NAS).

Ultimately, all these experiences helped both Ana and me depend on Him during the almost four years of separation by praying, fasting, and crying for answers. Without faith and trusting in Him, we could have given up. I could have possibly found another companion, and Ana could have done the same. However, I would have lived in guilt all my life for abandoning my wife and five children in Angola and for not working hard enough to get them back.

A thoughtful letter dated July 23, 1979 from US senator from Indiana, Birch Bayh, was received after our family reunification. He enclosed a copy of the reply he had received from the Department of State in response to his inquiry on my behalf. He wrote,

> I am very pleased that your family is being allowed to enter the United States. I know the waiting has been most difficult for all of you.

Thanks to God and His People

We gave thanks to God for leading Ana and me through hardships, challenges, and suffering that helped us develop endurance and character which gave us hope. "Not only so, but we also glory in our sufferings, because we know that suffering produces perseverance; perseverance, character; and character, hope. And hope does not disappoint us, because God's love has been poured out into our hearts through the Holy Spirit, who has been given to us" (Romans 5:3–4 NIV). These verses are repeated several times in our book because we depended so much and so often on them during many of our difficult circumstances.

We tried to thank all the people who were involved. We have learned that God often works through people by calling them and nudging them into action. God works in their hearts and lives so they can become His instruments for answering the prayers of others.

On the first Sunday of our family being reunited, we worshiped at the Community United Church of Christ whose members had been very supportive. Our entire family sang the following song in Portuguese:

> We've a story to tell to the nations
> That shall turn their hearts to the right
> A story of truth and mercy
> A story of peace and light
> A story of peace and light
> For the darkness shall turn to dawning. And the
> dawning to noonday bright. And Christ's great
> kingdom shall come to earth. The kingdom of
> love and light (Colin Sterne)

In the first few months, involved churches invited us to tell our story. We usually sang the song in Portuguese and then in English before I told of our experiences. We sang to praise God for greatness, wisdom, power, grace, and the mighty work of Redemption (Revelation 5:13–14). I was simply telling the story based on my appreciation of our awesome God for all He had done to reunite our family. While singing and sharing our experiences, I was overwhelmed by His magnificence and thought about, "Praise and glory and wisdom and thanks and honor and power and strength be to our God for ever and ever. Amen" (Revelation 7:12 NIV)! I always thanked the wonderful people who had helped us meet our physical and emotional needs. Psalm 105:1–5 (NIV) says, "Give thanks to the Lord, call on his name, and make known among the nations what he has done. Sing to him, sing praise to him; tell of all his wonderful acts… Remember the wonders he has done, his miracles."

On August 16, 1979, I sent letters of appreciation to Senator Birch Bayh and Mrs. Elise Tsomaia, the Social Services supervisor at the Immigration and Refugee Program (CWS) in New York. Also, I stayed in touch with the Immigration and Naturalization Service, based in Hammond, Indiana, regarding the annual whole family interviews.

Reunited Family Stays Busy

After our first total family worship in the United States, we had lunch with the family of Fred Dare. This seemed very appropriate for my family to enjoy the fine food, fellowship, and love that the Dares had provided so often to me. Our children's interest in sports expanded that day with them being introduced to baseballs and footballs. The Dare children played with them in the backyard.

There was a Vacation Bible School at Eden UCC the week after my family arrived. Member Beth Hall volunteered to transport our children to and from the Monday to Friday activities. I was in school, and Ana could not yet drive. Our children learned the songs in English very well. On Sunday, the day of presentation, our children sang along beautifully. This was their first time singing in English. The following week, the kids attended another Vacation Bible School at Community UCC.

Family Adjustments

This was a time of adjustment for all of us. My family had to adjust to the new environment, including the new language. The church family helped us find a family doctor, a dentist and a hygienist (Hennigars from Eden Church), and an ophthalmologist. Having the services of the doctor and dentist free was greatly appreciated, especially since our financial condition was a hardship at that time.

After two days, the Muncie newspaper followed up on our story, took a family picture, and published a family blog (not pictured in the book). People provided some financial help. We enrolled our children in the Muncie Community School System.

Life started to become normal little by little. I felt great relief to again have my wife and children. However, I had to manage lots of things simultaneously like enrolling the kids in school, arranging for Ana to learn the new language and maintain my college studies. Each member of our family had to move individually and collectively into the new society with a new language, foods, sports, and a diverse culture. God had a plan for our lives and future. "For I know the plans I have for you, declares the Lord, plans to prosper you and not to harm you, plans to give you hope and a future" (Jeremiah 29:11 NIV). God's plan is dynamic, not static. We always need to be proactive every day and follow His plan. Every day is a gift from God. As Max Lucado quoted, "God is at work in each of us, whether we know it or not, whether we want it or not."

A social worker friend from Eden UCC suggested that we apply for welfare assistance. So we signed up for the Food Stamps Program. Ana worked at the nursing home. I did part-time jobs at the university, such as being a custodian of our church in the evenings, etc. We decided that we had "enough" money to support the family without governmental assistance.

> God is at work in each of us, whether we
> know it or not, whether we want it or not. (Max
> Lucado)

We terminated our participation in the Food Stamps Program after eight months.

Our Education, Work and Life in the United States

Learning English, 1979

Anibal and Ana started at the Muncie Career Center studying English as a second language. Anibal (thirteen) graduated within six weeks with English proficiency and moved on to Storer Middle School. The boys were enrolled in schools. Azevedo (eleven), Cicero (nine), and Arlindo (seven) went to Mitchell Elementary School. The teachers were fabulous integrating them into the classes. Our children learned much from the teachers and from their peers. Clarisse (five) stayed home with her mom. After school, the boys watched *Sesame Street*, the American educational children's television series. We all appreciated the PBS station. Normally, after dinner, all the kids went to the playground and hung out with neighborhood kids. They kept learning new words, sentences, and American slang. They learned English and the American culture very quickly.

Conversely, Ana as an adult did not socialize as much with others, partly because of her difficulty understanding and speaking English. She went with Anibal to the Muncie Area Career Center. She stayed in the program for a year and eventually got her GED (the high school equivalent) certificate. Norma Carmichael sometimes brought children's books to help Ana learn new words and sentences. Somehow in one way or another, they could communicate by body language and gestures.

Ana Finds Work, 1980

Ana babysat five children of university students. On one hand, it helped her learn a few words and sentences. On the other hand, it was a burden added to having her own five kids after school. One mother took advantage of her. She would bring her son on Friday mornings and leave him until Monday afternoons without bringing extra clothes. Fortunately, we could lend him clothes since he was about Arlindo's size. We even took the boy to church on Sundays.

Pastor Don Orander (now deceased) of Eden UCC (Eden Church) visited us. He listened to our new life adjustments and felt compassion for Ana. He asked, "Does Ana know how to make a bed and to give a bath to an elderly person?" We said she could try. After a couple of days, he came back and took her to a local nursing home, Chateau. She started working there on a part-time basis. After one month, she got an employee of the month award and a bonus check of $50 because of her work ethic and diligence. Not only was it an honor, but the money also helped our family to meet our basic needs. (See picture in the middle of the book.)

Family Pictures

In Miapia-Bela Vista with Ana's parents,
Ana in middle (nine) in 1956.

At the church in Cavango Joe's parents, Ana and Anibal,
visiting my parents in September 1967.

In Cavango-Bela Vista with young Anibal in March 1967.

Visiting Benguela; my sister Joaquina (middle) and her family
in April 1974 (Clarisse getting ready to be born).

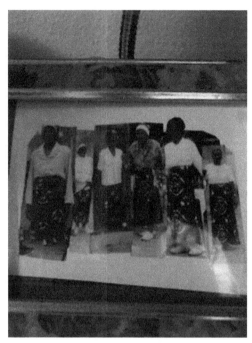

Ana's sisters and Mom; (from the left) Felicia, Madalena, Ilda, Mom Rosa, Marta, and Ana visiting her family in Huambo in 2004. (Mom died two years after.)

My only living sister, Julieta, and her husband, Benjamin Miguel. We visited Lubango, Angola, in 2016.

In Nova Lisboa, me as a sergeant in December 1964.

Joe's Father holding Azevedo

In Humpata, Huila Employee at Veterinary Institute in April 1969.

Back to Nova Lisboa in February 1970.

On our first Sunday at the Dare's home, Cicero was
amazed adjusting to the new environment and food.

Church directory picture in August 1980.

Grandchildren at the home of Arlindo in Indianapolis, 2008.

Grandchildren Indy in May 2009.

Fifteen grandkids in 2009–2018.

Wedding and Anniversaries

(Left) Cubal, Angola, with godparents, Vigario and Cacllda.
Rings exchanged on June 25, 1966; (right) signing the book.

Serving is the godmother, Cacilda; Ana, the bride
is in the middle, talking to a dignitary.

Fiftieth wedding anniversary at Noblesville First UMC, 2016

Church Family

Eden UCC Home Builders class at the Whitman's
in 1985 in Muncie annual party.

Rev. Don, retired, and Mary Jean Orander, of Eden UCC at their home in Indianapolis. Mary Jean holding Clarisse's son, David, 2005.

Reverend Fred, retired, and Nancy Dare of Community UCC and presently in Colorado Springs in 2014.

Mrs. Bryant and daughters Becky and Sherrell gave us individual gifts every Christmas. The picture shows Thanksgiving party at her house in Muncie in 1990.

Darrell and Barb Hockersmith, the former Angolan missionaries, retired, in Colorado Springs (1996)

The women of the Community UCC led by Sharon Brown, all the VBS, the first Sunday worshiping in USA at Community UCC, led by Sharon Brown (in the middle front row), Rosie Wells (right third row), and others. In the picture, one can see conspicuously Cicero close to Rosie, Arlindo, and Clarisse close to Sharon (Anibal and Azevedo are somewhere at the back row). In July 1979, women signed the card and raised $250. She sent both the card and the certified check to Ana while they were in Portugal in May 1979. It was a surprise!

Kathy Grile, leader at the youth choir performance at Eden
UCC with Chris Painter also in pictured, 1983

Kelli Brown talking to Kathy Grile and Nova Selvey
listening to the conversation. Clarisse's high school
graduation open house in our new home in 1993.

Journey to the USA

Joe with Dr. Jonas Savimbi,
president of UNITA political party in 1975.

Treasurer for UNITA in 1975.

Some Angolan students: (back) S. Paulo, Aarao, Jose, and Anacleto (front) Comigo, J. C. Paulino and M. Samondo.

Joe (third from the left) at Georgetown University studying in English as a second language program.

Picture taken by Larry Henderson;
family before leaving Huambo to Portugal in October 1977.

At Plymouth Church, Joe playing piano. Marcos, Anita, Sid Paulo,
Anacleto, Aaron Cornelio singing "When Peace First Sun."

Joe making the first call to Ana
at Ball State University in December 1977.

Deeply in thoughts
After talking to Ana

Joe in deep thinking after the call. "What's Next…"

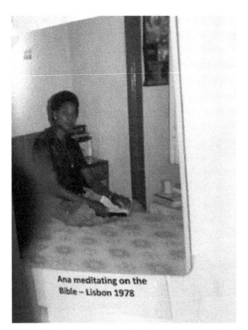

Ana meditating on the
Bible – Lisbon 1978

Ana's daily devotional before going to bed
(getting promises from the Lord).

Arlindo with a broken arm from a tax cab.
Getting love and support from his Mom.
Lisbon, April 1978.

Arlindo with a broken arm is surrounded by his
neighbors and friends in Lisbon, Portugal, 1978.

Joe leaving Capitol Hill; the first trip to DC with Rev. Fred Dare.

Joe and Rev. Fred Dare in DC in 1978.

First car, in USA in 1978.

BSU students David, Maliki, Abigal, Manuel
and his wife Ann, and Shadrack.

Fifty-plus people waiting! Singing at TWA Gate on July 22.

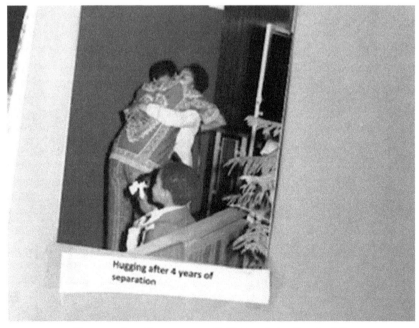

Hugging after 4 years of separation

"A nossa batalha erminou!" ("Our fight finished!")

Summary of the ("Family Reunited.")

Welcome to our new home in USA!

Second home, 1022 Rex St., Muncie; Ana working as a graduate assistant at Ball Memorial Hospital. She passed the state board exam in 1991!

Third home, 4401 University Avenue, Muncie,
(Lydia, future daughter-in-law) in 1992.

Awards and Scholarships

In October 1980, I received an award of $250 from the Department of Natural Resources, the Cooper's Science Award Selection for 1980–1981. The award says, "This award recognizes a student in each of the science departments at Ball State University who has demonstrated high moral and ethical behavior." My family attended the awards ceremony. The money was a significant amount for our family. (See Dr. Don Van Meter's picture at the end of the book.)

Later, I sent an application to the Angola Memorial Scholarship, based in Canada. Fortunately, my request for funding of continuing education was successful. I got $1,000 annually to pay tuition. My previous work with this organization likely helped me earn this very helpful financial award for both years of graduate school.

Our Challenges Continue, 1980 and Beyond

In 1980, I graduated from Ball State University with a major in natural resources and a minor in biology. (See pictures at the end of the book.) It was a joy to achieve this step after overcoming so many obstacles like family stress and fighting the Immigration and Naturalization red tape. Much had certainly changed during my four years earning a college degree in America. I no longer needed to expend so much energy trying to get my family safely here. Our faith, perseverance, and work had brought us amazing success through the guidance and love of God. We still had much uncertainty, but we were making progress together in our new environment.

I was now searching for employment to support my family, ideally in my area of study. I sent résumés and letters to companies and corporations in Indiana and elsewhere, but to no avail. To my surprise, I got responses telling me that they appreciated being contacted, but they did not have vacancies at the time but that they would consider me in the future. Sure! Then Pastor Dare and some members of his congregation suggested that I go to Houston and personally search for a job with the oil companies. I took the long bus trip. I stayed with friends of the Dares. I submitted job applications to several local companies. Unfortunately, I left Houston without any job offers. There were jobs in the National Parks for citizens not for a permanent resident as I classified at the time.

To financially sustain our daily living, I did odd jobs, such as working as a janitor with Ana at Eden United Church of Christ during the evenings. We cleaned the bathrooms, vacuumed the carpet in the sanctuary and on the hallways, and mopped and waxed the floors. To supplement the income, I worked at the Muncie IVY Tech as a janitor. I cleaned the public restrooms, mopped, waxed the floors, and took trash bags to the dumpsters.

Since I was having no success in securing a full-time job, I decided to go back to school to maintain the requirements for our living in the university family housing. Continuing to live at the university apartments was much cheaper than living off campus. I enrolled in education to become a teacher. While in school, I was working part-time at the university library showing films in classrooms. To pay my tuition, I secured a student loan. After a semester, I did student teaching at the local middle and high schools. My primary assignment was at Burris High School, where I taught biology. It was not easy to teach the students. Some of them made fun of my accent. During summers, I worked for the University Maintenance Housing Department cleaning and painting student apartments. I was very willing to do many odd jobs to help support our family. I never thought that I was too good to do any tasks required. Also I was always motivated to do them to the best of my ability just as my father had demonstrated long ago.

As I was showing a film about the future job market projections, I saw that computer science was the best career choice in the twenty-one-year trend. Something nudged in my heart, and I had a burning desire to go into the computer science area. I thought the pay would be much better than teaching. I went to the Computer Sciences Department to explore the requirements of a master's candidate. I was advised to take some prerequisite courses as an undergraduate before I would be considered as a master's candidate. I enrolled and got a job working as graduate assistant in the computer laboratories. I helped students with their assignments and supervised the lab. The little light came on at the end of the tunnel!

As a graduate assistant, I earned more money and did not have to show videos anymore. However, there was a catch-22. I had to maintain my grade point average at a B or better to keep the job as a graduate assistant. I had lots of pressure keeping up with my studies and finishing the computer projects after writing the codes. To accomplish this, the computer lab was my second home. Later, I regretted not assisting my family better, especially when the kids were growing up and adjusting to the new environment. I was basically trying to survive and could not do everything as well as I would have liked. Perfection was not possible.

> I was basically trying to survive and could
> not do everything as well as I would have liked.

I tried to maintain a B average, but in the computer languages course, the professor gave me a C. I panicked, and it scared me badly. Being confused and uncertain, I prayed to God to teach me and show me what to do next. "Call to me, and I will answer you and show you great and mighty things, which you don't know" (Jeremiah 33:3 NIV). To avoid having the C as a final grade, I had a nudge and decided to go and talk personally to the professor. I went to his home and begged him to consider it as an incomplete grade. I begged him to give me an extra assignment to raise the grade. He squarely refused to do either. "Oh my God!" I reacted. I was completely distraught. I remember leaving his house and sitting on the curb close to his driveway. I was despondent and sobbed bitterly like a small child, confused and not knowing what to do next. I went home and explained it to my best supporter and soul mate, Ana. We prayed together for God's guidance.

The next day, I explained my situation to Dr. Clinton Fueling, chairman of the Computer Sciences Department. Graciously, he listened and suggested that I repeat the course and that I could maintain my grad assistant job. I worked diligently by sleeping about four to five hours a night in order to study and do my computer assignments in the lab. My children hardly saw me at home during the week. Ana graciously understood my predicament and kept the home and family activities going despite being very busy also.

I continued singing in the choirs at both the churches. The pastors and the members continued to do much for us. Community gave us a newer car to replace our old one. A mother and her two adult daughters greatly helped our Christmas celebrations and joy. Every Christmas, they put envelopes (containing money) for each of us on the Christmas Tree. (See picture in the middle of the book.)

To keep up with the stress and health issues, Ana and I tried to be physically active. I exercised in a gym and in running races. Ana joined me in the lifestyle. The kids were involved in school sports, the soccer community, and the church youth activities.

Visiting Angolan Friends, 1980 and 1981

After I graduated from college and during a busy time of challenges and adjustments, we visited three Angolan families in Tucson, Arizona. Our financial situation was not good; but we needed a break and wanted to see relatives, friends, and more of the United States. To save money, we leased a compact car and took food from home.

The car was almost new but quite small. Clarisse (six) sat up front between Ana and me. Our four sons (fourteen, twelve, ten, and eight) were crowded in the backseat. We felt packed in the car like sardines in a can. However, no one minded sitting close together because we were looking forward to visiting our friends and relatives. We played cassette tapes of Michael Jackson most of the way. After traveling all day and half the night, we checked into a cheap motel where cockroaches also resided.

With my friend Anacleto and his family, we drove to the city of Nogales, on the Mexican border. Seeing the disparity between the two countries, we felt really blessed to be in the USA. After five days we came back home happy to have been away for the first time since the reunification of our family.

In 1981, we visited a family in Grove City, Pennsylvania. We planned to risk driving our old car, a 1954 Ford Fairlane. However, the day before leaving, Pastor Don Orander surprised us by offering the use of his primary car for our trip. He also brought a large cooler of cold drinks and snacks for our enjoyment and comfort. Wow! We were amazed and pleased that he would entrust his valued vehicle to us. (See picture in the middle of the book.) His generosity reminds me of the biblical scriptures: "Mary took about a pint of pure nard, an expensive perfume; she poured it on Jesus' feet and wiped his feet with her hair... It was worth a year's wages" (John 12:3, 5 NIV).

Reviewing Status with Immigration and Naturalization, 1982

My family and I were advised to be interviewed annually by the Immigration and Naturalization Service in Hammond, Indiana. This concerned extensions of our departure date. We certainly did not want to leave the United States and had no other country where we could legally live.

In 1982, I compiled copies of letters from friends and families in Angola and Portugal written in Portuguese and had them translated into English by a professor of foreign languages at Ball State University. We had the documents notarized. Most of the letters mentioned that Angola had become worse than in the colonial era. Food scarcity was serious, but continuing persecution of people belonging to UNITA was worse. The Luanda Regime routinely jailed or executed them. Based on this evidence, we were guaranteed permission to become permanent residents of the United States without needing to go back for interviews. My proactive efforts resulted in us knowing we could stay in the United States indefinitely. This was a huge milestone for us.

> Based on this evidence, we were guaranteed permission to become permanent residents of the United States without needing to go back for interviews.

Children's Achievements

Ana and I feel blessed with every child we have. Several of their formative and early years were in war-torn Angola and in poverty in Portugal, altogether being away from me for almost four years. When they finally arrived in the United States, their ages ranged from five to thirteen. All had to learn English and pursue their studies with peers whose first language was English. Our children had to quickly adapt to life in a new country and to a new culture. (See picture in the middle of the book.) All seemed to develop friendly, outgoing, and modest attitudes and personalities. They have always had excellent people skills or abilities to get along well with almost everyone. I have heard that people skills are more important than technical knowledge. All our children have good work ethics. They are motivated to treasure, support, and appreciate their families with love. We have always believed that God has blessed us greatly through our children.

All our kids worked hard and excelled in numerous ways. Some excelled in academics, others in sports. They were all involved in sports, such as T-ball, football, soccer, tennis, cross-country, track-and-field, wrestling, and volleyball. (Like their mom and dad, they are all runners. Seven of us from different states and cities planned and trained to run the Indy Mini [13.1 miles] in Indianapolis, Indiana, in 2002. Unfortunately, Anibal and his wife, Lydia, one week prior to the race, lost two twin baby girls. Lydia encouraged everyone to go ahead and run the race as planned to celebrate the short-lived lives. On the race day, all of us wore the t-shirts with a design: "Our Miracle Babies—Sarah, April 12–May 3, 2002 & Sayla, April 15–April 27, 2002.") (See picture at the end of the book). All of our children became long distance runners, and all four sons have run in at least one marathon (26.2 miles).

In church, they were active in the youth program and in the children's and youth choirs led by Kathy Grile. They sang in the Muncie Community Choir during the Christmas season. Sometimes, their names were published in the Muncie newspaper in recognition of achievements.

Acquiring soccer skills in Angola and Portugal, the three older boys were involved in a soccer club and on traveling teams. They taught several dribbling techniques to their American teammates. Anibal played in a higher skilled league and Azevedo and Cicero started in the intermediate level.

Azevedo (145 pounds), Cicero (152 pounds), and Arlindo (119 pounds) were involved in wrestling in Muncie North High School. One season, all three won the sectionals. The newspaper headline stated, "Three Chimbandas won the sectionals!" Also the same three played football at Muncie North High School (not pictured in the book).

Anibal excelled in high school and was usually on the honor roll. Besides the soccer club activities, he played tennis as a hobby. He went to Indiana University. He served in the army three years. He went back to school, specializing in X-ray technology. He is a radiology manager at a hospital. He is married and has two children. He ran in the Chicago Marathon. Being our oldest child, he provided much childcare for his siblings when they were very young.

Azevedo excelled in sports. Besides playing for the soccer club, he played football, wrestled, and ran cross-country and track. He won the Delaware County championships every year. He qualified to go to the state wrestling championships. After graduating from high school, he went to Lincoln Tech in Indianapolis and specialized in auto mechanics. Many years later, in the 2006 Chicago Marathon, when I ran it to qualify for the Boston Marathon, Azevedo demonstrated his natural running abilities. Although he had not trained as well as he would have liked, his skills enabled him to complete his first marathon. He is working at ZF Friederichshasfen AG as a machine operator in Lafayette, Indiana. He is married and has three children and one grandchild.

Cicero excelled in high school football, pole vaulting, and wrestling. He is our most fearless and adventurous child, having done scuba diving and sky jumping. In wrestling, he went to the state championships and won sixth place in his weight division. He has run in twelve marathons as of 2020. He went to an Indiana University Soccer Camp, where he was recruited by a scout to attend DePaul University, in

Chicago on a partial soccer scholarship. He graduated with a major in computer science. After graduation, he joined the International Church of Christ. He had a call from God and went into evangelism becoming a missionary. He worked in Johannesburg, South Africa, and planted churches and evangelized in the Portuguese community (refugees from Angola and Mozambique). After six months, he went to Maputo, the capital of Mozambique and Gaborone, Botswana, to continue evangelization for an additional ten months. He tried to do similar work in Angola but was not permitted. After returning to the United States, he worked for a couple of companies in Chicago supporting their computer networks. Currently (2020), he is a vice president in information technology at Loop Capital. He also teaches cybersecurity part time at a junior college in Chicago. He has one daughter.

Arlindo excelled in academics. He was in the Academic Honor Society. He volunteered in Kiwanis activities. He was in T-ball, Cub Scouts, football, and wrestling. He went to Ball State University majoring in accounting. He earned a John Fisher partial scholarship through Ball Corporation. He worked as a summer intern for Ball Corporation in its Accounting Department. After graduation, he worked at Price-Water-House Coopers, Deloitte & Touche LLP accounting firms and subsequently at Rolls-Royce Corporation. He ran in the Indianapolis Marathon. He is married and has four biological children and two adopted sons from Ethiopia. In 2020, he and his family moved to Atlanta, where he manages the Accounting Department at Jarden Home Newell Brands. Unfortunately, this move to Georgia took our closest family much farther away from us.

Clarisse in one year was involved in cheerleading, track-and-field, volleyball, school choir, and 4-H Club's Sewing and Baking projects. She was a special volleyball digger. She was recognized as the best defensive volleyball player at Muncie Central High School. She played for volleyball clubs which helped her develop her skills. She won a full-ride volleyball scholarship to Cleveland State University. We were blessed by not having to pay anything for her four-year education in physical therapy. She has run several half marathons (13.1 miles), and her goal is to run, at least, one marathon. She is married and has three children. She works as a physical therapist at the Outpatient Clinical in Bowie, Maryland.

With their involvement in sports, emphasis on education, and activeness in church, our kids have been able to pass on many of our family traditions and values to their children, our precious grandchildren.

Grandchildren's Achievements

Our parents taught that education, faithfulness to God, and hard work were extremely important to us and every aspect of our lives. They taught us how to fish rather than giving us a fish. Now our children are working to teach their kids the same values as well as to prepare them to meet the inevitable challenges of life by both faith and works. They emulate the apostle Paul advising a young Timothy: "But as for you, continue in what you have learned and have become convinced of, because you know those from whom you learned it, and how from infancy you have known the holy Scriptures, which are able to make you wise for salvation through faith in Christ Jesus" (2 Timothy 3:14 NIV).

Our grandchildren love God, singing, sports, and running. We regret that distance and other things prevent us from seeing and supporting them as much as we would like. However, we realize and appreciate that our families must be mobile and live their own lives. Even though we can't see them often, we like to believe that the accomplishments of our children and grandchildren are tributes to us and our ancestors.

As of 2020, Isaiah (thirty) with his son Josiah (three) and Elisha (twenty-five) love basketball and working. Simeon (twenty-three) is focusing on finishing his college and working. Naja Rosa (twenty-two) graduated from college with honors in special education. Jonas (twenty-one) is studying civil engineering at the University of Dayton, where he runs cross-country and track. Sophie (nineteen) is at Duke University. She has a passion for social justice issues and is involved in the Kenan Institute of Ethics. Yoni (eighteen) runs cross-country and track in high school. Alex (seventeen) plays on a varsity soccer team in high school. Jonathan (seventeen) is president of his class, plays soccer, and runs track in high school. Carolina (fifteen) plays soccer and the tenor saxophone and is fluent in Portuguese. David (fifteen) is fluent in French and plays football in high school. Ella (fourteen) earned academic awards and runs cross-country at her middle school. Lilly (thirteen) loves art and painting. She sings in her school choir. Caleb (thirteen) is also fluent in French, is active in the student council, and plays soccer and the violin. Saraia (five) is busy keeping up with her two brothers and looking forward to starting kindergarten. (See pictures in the middle of the book.)

We believe that "the sky is the limit" for our grandchildren, their children, and beyond. Although we won't be privileged to witness all their challenges, actions, and accomplishments, we hope they realize how honored we are to have them as Chimbanda descendants, taking our DNA into the future. We believe that many of our past activities involved divine help, enabling us and our descendants to not only exist but to make our world a better place to live and prepare for the next. With my legacy of running, an analogy of us passing the baton on to future generations seems appropriate.

My Graduation and Moving Out of Family Housing, 1984

In August 1984, I graduated with a master of arts in computer sciences. Praise the Lord for one more success in life! (See pictures at the back of the book.) I started putting resumes in the job market. With a degree in computer sciences, I thought I would quickly get a job. Unfortunately, this was not the case. It seemed nothing was easy.

Since I had graduated, we had to vacate University Family Housing. A member of the Community UCC suggested that we rent a house he had available. (See picture in the middle of the book.) We rented it but regretted the decision. Being close to the university campus gave us weekend headaches. From Thursday to Sunday evenings, the students partied outside with loud music and used our front yard for littering. We found many empty beer cans and cigarette butts. To make it worse, we could hardly use the basement because it flooded whenever it rained. Still, we were thankful for the upward step of living in a house. We had been unable to live in our own house since our "bubble broke" in Angola several years earlier.

My Professional Job, 1984

A great friend and member of the Eden UCC, Norma Carmichael, empathized with our difficulties and contacted an editor of the Muncie Star regarding our situation. The newspaper person Rita Winters (deceased) arranged for a family picture and an interview for the story. An excellent article resulted. Our children played soccer with children of the top leaders of Ball Corporation. After seeing the newspaper story, the leaders asked me to interview for a job. Norma Carmichael's thoughtful initiative in suggesting the newspaper story led to an amazing opportunity.

Since I needed employment so much, I prepared extensively for the interview. I explored Ball Corporation's culture, history, and successes. The interview went very well, and I was offered a job as a computer programmer. Regarding preparation, Peter exhorted Christians by saying, "Always be prepared an answer to everyone who asks you to give the reason for the hope that you have" (1 Peter 3:15 NIV).

This was a professional job with a very prestigious company! Also, I was the first African American in its Information Technology Department. When I started work, I learned that a couple of my new coworkers were not pleased that I was there. I am a person who likes to greet everyone I encounter. When I would meet them and said hello, they would ignore me. I kept saying hello to them to stay free of guilt in my heart. I was reminded of Jesus saying, "You have heard that it was said, 'Love your neighbor and hate your enemy.' But I tell you, love your enemies and pray those who persecute you" (Matthew 5:43–44 NIV). I kept praying for them. When we moved to Denver, Colorado, about fourteen years later, one of them moved with me and became the "best friend ever." Prayers work! People often asked me how I got the job and told me how fortunate I was. I suspect some divine help was involved, and I certainly realized how fortunate I was.

I worked in a support role for the Accounting Department using the computer language called COBOL, acronym for Common Business-Oriented Language. I mainly wrote codes for new programs and made changes in the old programs based on changes in business, finance, and administrative tasks. After two years, I moved to a department supporting the Payroll and Human Resources Departments. I designed and wrote a programming code for new payroll checks and stubs.

I greatly appreciated my employment and was a dedicated, hardworking employee. After seven years with the company, I was promoted to senior programmer. Ball Corp treated its employees well and rewarded achievements. We really enjoyed their Christmas parties and summer picnics. (See picture at the end of the book.)

The Ball brothers had brought their businesses and entrepreneurial spirit to Muncie many years earlier to utilize natural gas that was abundant for a while. Ball canning jars and the Hubble telescope were among their claims to fame. Their support and name were provided to Ball State University, Ball Memorial Hospital, and the Ball Foundation, all very important assets to Muncie and Indiana. It was Indiana's loss and Colorado's gain when the company headquarters moved to Denver. Although we did not want to leave our Muncie friends, I was pleased and honored to have been asked to transfer with my employer to another state.

Ana Faces College Challenges

As mentioned previously, Ana got a job at the Chateau Nursing Home, where she worked hard and earned money to supplement our income. Then she found a job at the West Minister Village Nursing Home with better pay. However, the work was so physically demanding that she hurt her back from lifting heavy loads and patients. After careful thought, we decided that she should resume her education. She earned her GED diploma at the Muncie Career Center. She enrolled in English classes at Ball State University as a part-time student. She reduced her working hours.

After about a year, she applied to Ball State and started taking courses as a prenursing student. After taking all the prerequisite courses, she entered the nursing program. The classes were difficult. The science courses were not as hard as the English language classes and other liberal art courses that needed a strong knowledge of English. In 1984, she got an honor certificate as recognition for achieving a 3.0 grade point average (GPA) from the Ball State University Minority Student Development.

One of her closest church friends suggested that Ana take courses to become a licensed practical nurse. First, she said that it would be faster to finish and have a degree. Secondly, it would be easier than pursuing the four-year RN program because of the language difficulties. Ana said no, having already completed many of the required science courses for the nursing program. The change would be failing toward her dream. Then the lady said, "Oh, I think you know what you want and are determined to do for your life." Ana believed the promise of Philippians 1:6 (NIV), which states, "Being confident of this, that he who began a good work in you will carry it on to completion."

As Ana moved forward, classes became much harder. Her GPA decreased. First, being a mother of five children and taking care of the household and family responsibilities were big factors. Secondly, she was competing with younger and intelligent students whose first language was English. The class had about 180 nursing students. She was unable to take good lecture notes because of the language barriers. She spent many hours reading the material from books, but the tests included questions from both the books and lectures. Therefore, she could not score well on the exams.

Choices for Ana, 1984

One day, one of the professors approached Ana and invited her to the office to provide some advice. She said, "Ana, I know you want to get a nursing degree, but to tell you the truth (1) we need only eighty students from this class to continue with the nursing program, (2) your grades are not high enough to be selected, (3) you have

English communication barriers that will prevent you from completing the program and then passing the state board exams. But I have an alternative. You should transfer to Marion College (now Indiana Wesleyan University), which is a Christian College and has a high number of international students. They would help you with your studies since the college is smaller than Ball State." This advice was very difficult to accept, but time proved it to be correct.

Ana cried, cried, and cried. But looking back, she was reminded, "Those who sow in tears shall reap with joyful shouting" (Psalm 126:5 NAS). She came home and talked with me about the situation. We decided to drive to Marion College so that she could memorize the route to drive there by herself without getting lost. At that time, there were no GPS or cell phones. We did not know how to navigate very well. Therefore, she memorized the road signs and exits. We drove to Marion the next day without any problems. People sometimes underestimate others' potential and determination. God reminded Samuel, "The Lord does not look at the things man looks at. Man looks at the outward appearance, but the Lord looks at the heart" (1 Samuel 16:7 NIV). Both Ana and I had gone through trials and tribulations and acquired a strong faith and trust in God for any circumstances. We knew the road ahead would be hard and even painful to follow. However, the Word of the Lord says, "No discipline seems pleasant at the time, but painful. Later on, however, it produces a harvest of righteousness and peace for those who have been trained by it" (Hebrews 12:11 NIV).

Early the next Monday, Ana drove our Chevrolet-Chevette to Marion College. She went directly to the Admissions Office Building to get information about the nursing program. The secretary gave her the details of whom she should contact. Then she went to meet Dr. Rebecca B. Ellis (deceased), the director of the nursing program. With her limited English, Ana explained her situation, and Dr. Ellis was very attentive, positive and sympathized with her situation. She said, "I can help you… Go back to Ball State, and get your transcript and bring it to the Admission Office so they can evaluate the courses you have taken. You might lose some credits, but don't worry, and we will go from there."

The following day, she went to Ball State and followed Dr. Ellis's advice. She met all the requirements. The following week, Ana was informed that she was approved to enroll in Marion College. Hurray! We celebrated this big achievement with the whole family.

Ana registered for the fall semester to start at Marion College (Wesleyan University) in 1986. Since I had a good job, we bought a new Colt Vista minivan. Our Chevette was old but drivable and smaller with good gas mileage. The car was perfect for Ana to commute to Marion College, about a one-hour drive each way.

Transition to Marion College, 1986

On the first day of the school, Dr. Ellis gave Ana a study plan. She also hired a student who needed financial aid to assist Ana. The student would take notes of the class lectures. After the classes, they would review and compare notes. She was almost a tutor. She helped Ana see things from a different perspective. Looking back, Ana realized with His infinite power, God could turn the most difficult of circumstances into something beautiful. We remembered one of our favorite verses of the Bible, "Those who hope in the Lord will renew their strength. They will soar on wings like eagles; they will run and not grow weary, they will walk and not be faint" (Isaiah 40:31 NIV).

After high school graduation, Azevedo enrolled in an auto mechanics program at Lincoln Tech in Indianapolis. He secured a school loan for the two-year program. Since he did not have transportation, he would drive his mom to Marion, drop her off, and drive to Indianapolis. In the evening, he would reverse the route. This routine was followed for almost two years. It was a challenge for all of us, but we needed to make sacrifices to keep making progress. Certainly. God was with them during their numerous trips. Ana said, "It was harder when it rained or snowed, especially driving a small car beside or behind semis."

Life at Marion College

Ana met an African American student in the same year of the nursing program. Anita was married and had two sons. She was a little younger than Ana, but they had much in common. She was a very nice, outgoing, and generous person. Together, they created strong bonds of friendship. Anita also commuted from near Muncie, so she was able to help provide transportation for Ana. Anita and Ana hung out and graduated together. After their state board exams, Anita was hired at Riley Hospital in Indianapolis. Unfortunately, several years later, when we lived in Denver, we learned that Anita had been hit by a drunken driver and found dead in her car. It was very tragic for Ana to think about the life they had gone through together. Looking back, while stranded in Portugal, Ana and our children were living with a generous Portuguese family when Jorge, the husband and family breadwinner, died from a sudden heart attack. Both these were huge losses in Ana's life. She could not understand why these terrible deaths occurred, but she had to accept them as part of life. Proverbs 16:9 (NIV) came to mind: "The mind of man plans his way. But the Lord directs his steps."

Ana's Graduation, 1991

In May 1991, Ana graduated from the nursing program with a bachelor of science registered nurse degree. Some people could not believe her achievement. They were like Thomas of the Bible! She had a pin ceremony wearing a white dress and a hat the night before graduation. Friends from our church and others went to the ceremony. Ana wore a black graduation gown and a black hat and tassel to get her certificate. Tears were streaming down the cheeks of Ana, her friends, and me. There were shouts, "Viva, hurray, Ana, Ana, Ana, you made it!" These were certainly tears and shouts of joy. "Tears of joy will stream down their faces, and I will lead them home with great care. They will walk beside quiet streams and on smooth paths where they will not stumble" (Jeremiah 31:9–13 NLT). (See pictures at the end of the book.) The Home Builders Class from our church at Eden brought a big cake and fruit punch to our house, so we continued the celebration with friends afterward. (See picture at the end of the book.)

State Board Exam

The battle was not over. Ana had another big challenge to face—the state board exam. Dr. Ellis, the nursing director, suggested that Ana enroll in a week review session. The cost was $180, which Ana borrowed from a bank. She and her friend, Ella, studied together for a week. Ella drove them to Indianapolis for the exams. In their hotel, they crammed for the test and prayed for good outcomes because Ella was also a believer.

After breakfast, they drove to the Convention Center in a big conference room for the exams. There were about a thousand students from Indiana. The paper exams were handed out to each student, and the test instructions were covered. Ana was overwhelmed with the environment. Her feelings ran the gamut from excitement to anxiety. "What if I don't do well? How would I pay for another review?" However, the review gave her assurance and confidence.

The two-day state board exams were not computerized at that time. Perhaps, that caused them to take so much time before giving the results.

Graduate Nurse at Ball Memorial Hospital

Ana, like other graduates, was hired as a graduate nurse at Ball Memorial Hospital while awaiting exam results. Ana still had some difficulty communicating in English but had high skills working with her hands. She was loved by others due to her personality, reasoning, humbleness, patience, compassion, and diligence. "If the ax is dull and its edge unsharpened, more strength is needed but skill will bring success" (Ecclesiastes 10:10 NIV).

During the time of waiting, there were two other graduate nurses in her unit. One was a very smart, tall, slim blonde who bragged that she was an A student. She was attracted to the staff, including the doctors. The manager presumed and prepared her to be a nurse-in-charge once she got her board exam certificate. After a few months, the exam results started coming one by one. Unfortunately, this girl did not pass, so she had to repeat the exam later. The second graduate nurse received the results that she had failed but did not give the information to Human Resources. She was asked repeatedly whether she had gotten her results. She lied in order to extend her job as a graduate nurse. Suspicious leaders eventually called the state board and learned that she had failed. She was not only dismissed from work but was banned indefinitely from retaking the exam.

Ana was scared when she learned that the other students had failed their exams. She waited for the mail every day and prayed. She instructed the kids to watch the mail at home for her results. If they saw a small brown envelope, it presumably would contain a passing certificate. A big brown envelope would likely contain a failing letter plus instructions of how to retake the exam.

Azevedo happened to be at home and got the mail. In the pile, he saw a small brown envelope. He called Ana and said, "Mom, I have a small brown envelope." Her uncertain situation was similar to the disciples who were praying for Peter when he was in prison by the King Herold,

> So Peter was kept in the prison, but prayer for him was being made fervently by the church of God… And when Peter knocked at the door of the gate, a servant girl named Rhoda came to answer. And when she recognizes Peter's voice, because of her joy she did not open the gate, but ran in and announced that Peter was standing in front of the gate. And they said to her, "You are out of your mind!"… And they kept saying "It is his angel." (Acts 12:5, 13–16 NIV)

The disciples fervently prayed, and God answered their prayers, but they were still astonished.

Of course, the small envelope caused Ana to be confident, but her heart was still beating wildly when she said, "Open it!" Azevedo opened it and said, "Mom, you passed!" Like the disciples, Ana was still astonished that her prayers had been answered. What excitement after finding out! She had scored 75 percent when 74 percent or below was a failing grade. She called me right away at work to tell me the good news. We celebrated well! (See picture in the middle of the book.) She called Ella, her study partner, and found that she had also passed. The exam review likely enabled them to pass, so the money had been well spent. Their hard work and prayers had brought success.

Ana's First Job as a Registered Nurse

After presenting her state board certificate at the hospital, Ana was offered a bonus of $2,500 to work as a registered nurse at Ball Memorial Hospital. Our lives were better from then forward.

Ana was assigned to the Telemetry Unit. During the summer, some professors of nursing worked at the hospital during their summer break from teaching. By coincidence, the professor who told Ana to change her major because of the English language barriers was assigned to Ana for orientation in that unit. Both were stunned. The professor thought Ana would never graduate from nursing school, much less pass the state board exam. On the other hand, Ana never thought she would ever supervise her former professor. Ana felt privileged to work with her, never mentioning the old advice. In the meantime, Ana thought she was returning a favor. They became close friends for the whole summer.

Purchasing a New House, 1992

We needed a better house. We found a nice modern home with four bedrooms, kitchen, living room with a fireplace, dining room, plus two and a half baths. (See picture in the middle of the book.) It was located three miles from Ana's work and six miles from mine. It was in a nice, quiet neighborhood. Our closest neighbors were a medical doctor and a pastor. The hard work, perseverance, and determination were resulting in much progress.

For the first time, we bought new furniture for our master bedroom, dining room, and living room, plus a lawn mower. Ana loved decorating the house and kept it impeccable. Many of our American friends admired the neatness and coziness of the house. Some of them were curious and asked which type of house we had in Angola.

Life like a Roller-coaster Ride

With the bonus money, Ana decided to reward herself by buying a new car. We drove to Indianapolis, where she purchased a Hyundai minivan. We had reached a comfort zone, another high point in our roller-coaster lives.

In retrospect, we concluded that our lifestyle had made a complete cycle. Back in 1969 in Angola, I had an excellent and highly respected job. Ana had finished nursing school and worked as nurse in a major hospital in Huambo. We had our own house and car. One child went to an expensive private school. We were living as upper-middle-class people, definitely a high point with several low points to soon follow.

That "bubble had burst." The Portuguese government had collapsed, and the Angolan civil war erupted. The civil war eventually wiped out our possessions. My family was fortunate to have escaped without injury or worse. With much prayer, effort, and help, we were all able to come to the United States but with essentially no material possessions. In America, we had to rebuild our lives. We learned a new language, returned to school, got good jobs, raised strong children, and eventually retired. Our lives seemed like a roller-coaster ride with lots of ups and downs. I discovered that we should never give up, because God never gives up on us. In fact, He will be the power source for our rides of life if we will permit it. Life is short but with much to discover and learn in the high and the low territories.

Eden United Church of Christ, 1979–1997

Many leaders and members of Eden UCC (now Eden Church) supported and celebrated our efforts to reunite our family. We worshipped there where we had many close friends. I served as financial secretary and on the Nominating Committee. Having appreciated the generosity of Church World Service, I volunteered to lead the CROP Hunger Walk. I also sang in the chancellor choir. Occasionally, I was invited to be a liturgist. We belonged to the Home Builders Sunday School Class whose members were close brothers and sisters. We learned so much from them about a new life and how to pursue our dreams in America. The biblical scriptures say, "As iron sharpens iron so one person sharpens another" (Proverbs 27:17 NIV). (See picture in the middle of the book.)

Norma Carmichael was the teacher of the Sunday School class. She was a bold, compassionate, and caring spiritual leader as well as an organizer and Bible scholar. She organized and conducted numerous class trips, retreats, and trips.

The Possum trips (as they were called) were popular for Eden Church youths and adults. On them, just before bedtime, the buses would be transformed into their sleeping mode. We were like baby opossums sleeping in our mother bus's pouches while extra drivers took us many miles toward more enjoyable places. I really enjoyed the food, fun, and fellowship. We were all just a big family living very close together for several days. I participated on one Possum trip while Ana was working very hard in college. A game caused me to suddenly realize that exact date was our wedding anniversary. As soon as possible, I called Ana fearing that she would be upset at my forgetting it. She had been so busy that she had not realized it either, so I was off the hook. With so much time on the bus, we played cards and did lots of things. We would get slap happy, laughing at everything whether actually funny or not. I remember that Ken Catron (now deceased) and I jumped up to give one another a "high five" to celebrate something. We were so tired that our hands missed touching by about a foot, setting off another explosion of laughter. All our children remember the trips. Being relatively new to the United States, they appreciated the natural beauty and fun of new places, as well as the togetherness of living so closely with Eden friends for several days.

Our children were also very appreciative of many meaningful church activities led by Kathy Grile and others. (See pictures in the middle of the book.) In 2020, Kelli Carmichael Brown wrote a note to Kathy that describes well the experiences of her and our children. Kelli wrote,

> I know you [Kathy] had better things to do than to spend a weekend in early October at Isanogel with a bunch of teenagers. But you created for us some of the most treasured memories of our lives. Through many youth leaders, you were our constant. You were truly Christ in action for us, and we are who we are as adults because of who you were for us when we were young. "Thank You."

The amazing Possum trips were an outreach mission of Taylor University in nearby Upland Indiana. They evolved from their Wandering Wheels Bicycle Mission.

Now that we are again living in Indiana, we see many of the present and past Home Builders Class members each year at a late-summer potluck and birthday celebration for Norma Carmichael. These are usually hosted by our good friends, Pat and Mike Thompson.

Gardening

We chose gardening as a hobby. We recalled our parents growing vegetables and other produce in their gardens and orchards. Family Housing at Ball State University provided garden plots for students and professors. We grew carrots, green beans, tomatoes, kale, peas, etc. We tilled the soil with a hoe, which was hard work. A professor named Ken saw me working very hard and sweating as I used the hoe. He said, "Joe, I have been seeing you working too hard. I have a rototiller you can use if you like." I replied, "Oh no, thanks, anyway. We do this as part of our exercise!"

Some of the vegetables like green beans and tomatoes were so plentiful that we canned them for the winter, likely using Ball jars of which Ball Corporation (my future employer) was famous. We have continued our gardening up to 2020. We enjoy eating fresh vegetables not only because they are delicious but also because we save money on our groceries.

As of 2020, we volunteer at our church's Teter Organic Farm. This farm was donated in 1981 by an active member of our church, Noblesville United Methodist Church. The church uses the 120-acre farm as a community outreach ministry to feed spirits, minds, and bodies in Hamilton County. Ana and I volunteer to start the seeds, plant, pull the weeds, and harvest. (See picture at the middle of the book.)

Becoming Citizens of the United States, 1994

In 1994, Ana and I reviewed the laws and the government in a booklet, *The Declaration of Independence Constitution of the United States Constitution of Indiana*. On May 24, we and Arlindo and Clarisse went to the United States District Court in Indianapolis. Along with many, we took the Oath of Allegiance and were sworn in as citizens of the United States of America. Our other sons became citizens later.

This was a major milestone for us. It was so special that I wanted to do something extraordinary and memorable. I thought back to my parents changing their names when they became Christians. I decided to change my name from Jose Chimbanda to Joseph John Chimbanda. Since then, I have been using the new name, Joseph John, rather than Jose. When my friends forget or don't know of the official change, I am certainly not bothered by being called Jose as I was known for about fifty years.

Changing names was prominent in the Bible. God changed Abram's "high father" to Abraham "father of a multitude" (Genesis 17:5) and Sarai "my princess," to Sarah "mother of nations" (Genesis 17:16–17). Jacob, after wrestling with God, demanded a blessing, and from then on, he was called Israel, meaning "one that struggled with the divine angel" (Genesis 32:28). After his dramatic conversion, Saul became Paul (Acts 13:9). Paul wrote much of the New Testament, providing several of our quotes about struggling and persistence.

Integrity Award, 1996

I was honored to receive a Delaware County Integrity Award. I was among five adults and nine students receiving these. The awards are to recognize high integrity and good character via ethical decisions based on strong values. I felt especially pleased because our Pastor Kenneth Crouch had nominated me.

Ball Corporation Moving to Denver, 1997

In late 1996, the president of Ball Corporation announced that its headquarters would be moved from Muncie to Denver. Ball Corp had an aerospace company located in Boulder, Colorado, so they decided to move the headquarters closer. They selected a few employees to relocate. Many of us were very worried that we would not be selected. I was apprehensive until I saw my name on the list. I was pleased in that it showed that I was appreciated. Again, we did not want to leave Muncie and our friends but needed to keep the excellent job. Our decision was easier in that all our children were married and were living in their own homes. Our friends in the Home Builders Sunday School Class threw a farewell party for us and our families as we headed to a new state. (See picture at the end of book.)

The company leaders arranged for employees and their spouses to secure housing in Denver. They assigned realtors to sell the Muncie homes and to help find houses in Denver. We were allowed to buy a house or to have a new one built. Ana and I could not find one that appealed to us. We had a new one built in Thornton, about ten miles from downtown Denver, with considerable financial assistance from the company.

Our October 1997 move to Colorado was eventful. Since our house had not been finished, we had the movers place our possessions in storage. We rented an apartment. Finally, on December 23, we had the movers transport the furniture and boxes to our new house. We spent Christmas unpacking and preparing our new house to become our home. We were very grateful that the company paid all the relocation expenses.

A person was assigned to help Ana prepare her résumé. She was soon hired full-time at the North Suburban Hospital and part-time on weekends at the Boulder Community Hospital.

Finding a church took time and effort. We found no United Church of Christ that met our selection criteria. We wanted a home church that had a choir and Sunday School classes and that was geographical close enough to permit us to be active on committees, choir practices, and other worship and service activities. We joined a United Methodist church just three miles from our house. It had about 150 members and met all our criteria. Ana joined the women's program and choir. (See picture at the end of the book.) I joined the chancellor choir and became active on several committees. After a couple of years, Ana and I successfully introduced the CROP Hunger Walk. We started the project with five walkers and a few donors. It has been growing well in the numbers of walkers and the amount of funds raised. In 2019, they celebrated their twenty-year anniversary and had twenty walkers and had tripled the amount of funds raised. We were honored to be mentioned as the ones who suggested that they start this very worthy project.

From Being Blessed to Being a Blessing

We have been so blessed to have had so many people help us. There is no way we can know and personally thank them all. We hope that what we do for others helps repay what others did for us. We helped Corey (age seven) fight his cancer as described later in the 1995 marathon section. We assisted our extended family by sponsoring two nieces to study in the United States and a niece in Angola.

During our first visit to our relatives in Angola in 2000, my sister Juliana was very sick with renal failure, and her husband was blind. We decided to help one of their six children continue his or her education. We asked them to select the one. They chose Etna Luvinga Sacato, their third child. We came back to the United States and handled her documentation. She came here in 2001. She started with English as a second language, just as we had over twenty years previously. She graduated from the nursing program in the University of Wyoming. When she went back to Angola, she got a job in one of the hospitals in Luanda and got married. She has been helping some of her nieces in Angola. We are very pleased with Etna.

In 2004, Ana visited her mom, who was very sick with no hope of recovery because of her age. When Ana had been back here for a few months, she got a call from Adalgiza Bonifacio, her great niece in Angola. Adalgiza had finished high school but was unable to continue her education. She wanted to get a college degree in the United States but could not afford it. We decided to do the same for her as we were doing for Etna. She soon joined Etna at University of Wyoming and graduated in computer science. She met someone at the university and got married. She has been financially helping her mom in Angola. It seems that most whom we help appreciate our efforts and then repay us by helping others.

In 2014, Ana and I went back to Angola to visit relatives. We arranged for four of Ana's orphaned relatives (ages six, eight, ten, and twelve) to be admitted to an orphanage. As of 2020, they are all happy and doing well in school. My nephew's grandchild manages the orphanage with his work being a very important mission. (See pictures of the orphan boys at the end of the book.)

Also we learned that one of Ana's nieces, Rosa, was struggling financially with her family. So we convinced our church's outreach program to help one of her children, Clarisse (named after our daughter), continue her education beyond high school. The outreach program and the church women's group are sponsoring Clarisse to study in Angola. As of 2020, she is a second-year law student at a university in Huambo, Angola. (See picture at the end of the book.) Also while living in Denver, we hosted our friend's daughter from Eden Church in Muncie during her internship with the Colorado Rapids Soccer team in Denver, Colorado.

We believe our coming to the United States had a purpose for God to use us for His glory. God told Abram, "Leave your country, your people and your father's household and go to the land I show you. I will make you into a great nation and I bless you…and you will be a blessing" (Genesis 12:1–2 NIV). We regret that our financial situation does not allow us to do as much as we would like. There are many heartbreaking unmet needs of children in Angola. Similar to Cornelius in the Bible, "Cornelius, a centurion…and all his family were devout and God-fearing; he gave generously to those in need and prayed to God regularly" (Acts 10:2 NIV). Ana and I strive to be devoted Christians and believe in generosity and in prayers. When we help others directly or through our readers, friends, and relatives, it is like passing on the baton to others.

Helping Build a Church in Angola, 2002

In September 2002, a team of seven men built a church in Angola. I took twenty days of vacation from work to help and interpret. Darrell Hockersmith, a long-time missionary in Angola, and his son Paul (builder) were leaders. The building materials were purchased by team members in Colorado Springs. My church sent me off with prayers and blessings.

We flew from Denver to Atlanta, Johannesburg, Windhoek, and then Lubango, Angola. (An added blessing was seeing my sister Julieta and her family, who lived there.) Paul and I flew to Luanda, the capital city, to investigate potential church building sites while the rest of the team drove to a couple churches that the team had built during a previous trip (Tombua and Virei).

We reconnected in Lubango and drove south about eight hours with our building materials to Xangongo City, district of Cunene. There, we built a new church structure near the River Cunene. The congregation, which had been worshipping under a big tree, was eager to help and enabled us to build the church in about one week. Upon completion, we placed church benches that we brought with us in the new building. The congregation was very happy and pleased to have a dedicated church building in which to gather and worship. (See picture at end of the book.)

We had devotions every morning before breakfast. We had a good cook in the group, so we ate well. At night, we slept in our sleeping bags outdoors at the construction site. Fortunately, there was no rain that week. Our repellents worked well against the many mosquitos near the river. The clear night sky displayed much of God's beauty: the Milky Way, full moon, and many stars. This reminds me of the biblical scriptures: "The heavens declare the glory of God; the skies proclaim the work of His hands" (Psalm 19:1 NIV).

After completing our work in Xangongo, we continued driving south to the first church building that had been built in Ondjiva. We quickly installed a ventilator in the roof and continued on to cross the border into Namibia.

In Namibia, we visited Etosha National Park, where we saw God's creations, including various wild animals. We drove back to Windhoek, Namibia. Then we flew from Windhoek to Johannesburg and then back to Denver. It was a blessing to help and interpret in support of the Angolan Mission Project in my native land.

Roller-coaster Circumstances Continue, 2004

In 2004, Ball Corporation in Colorado started dismissing employees from various departments to save money. Information technology outsourced many services, causing some positions to no longer be needed. Six employees from senior system analysts to programmer analysts were dismissed and offered a severance package. Unfortunately, my position as a senior programmer analyst was affected.

At the end of work one Friday, I was notified by my supervisor to report to the manager of the Human Resources Department. Being the first person to be dismissed, I had no clue what was happening. (This was like our low point when Ana had been called to the office of the director of the nursing programs as the first student removed from the program. The program could take only 80 of the 180 students in her class.)

The Human Resources director and an employee counselor told me, "Joe, your position has been terminated, sorry!" I retorted, "What! What did I do, my God?" It was like an atomic bomb falling on me! I was dejected. This was certainly a low point for me. They offered me three options: (1) they would send my family back to Muncie with all expenses paid by the company; (2) they would find someone to help me write a résumé to find a job in another company; or (3) they would offer me an open job in the administration support company as a mailroom specialist with no change in salary or in benefits. However, I would never receive any salary increases. I called Ana to give her the bad news.

What! What did I do, my God!

They gave me two weeks to tell my family and decide. We cried on the phone and then told our kids individually. Again we remembered about the hymn originally written by preacher Joseph M. Scriven, "What a friend we have in Jesus. All our sins and griefs to bear! What a privilege to carry. Everything to God in prayer." We took it to the Lord in prayer during the two weeks.

> What a friend we have in Jesus. All our
> sins and griefs to bear! What a privilege to carry.
> Everything to God in prayer. (Joseph M. Scriven)

Being age fifty-nine (official age), with a 401k and an accrued pension, we decided that I should stay with Ball Corporation until retirement. After two weeks, I told them I would accept the offered position. It was a hard adjustment to bear facing my friends and former coworkers in the Information Technology Department. However, they were very sympathetic and encouraged me to keep going. Unfortunately, the frozen salary impacted my future social security benefits.

My work in the mail room was quite different from what I had done as an information technology programmer. The adjustment was difficult, but administrative support from remarkable people helped me endure the new hardships. Julie Johnson, a longtime friend and former secretary of Eden UCC, had fortunately joined Ball Corporation in Denver. Mike Dillie and Diane Fasset, gurus of the mailroom; Paula Stanley, manager; and others in the department were very helpful to my challenging adjustment. To endure, I wrote and posted a sign from 1 Colossians 3:23–24 (NIV): "Whatever you do, work at it with all your heart, as working for the Lord, not for human masters, since you know that you will receive an inheritance from the Lord as a reward." This was certainly my dad's attitude. The concluding years of my career were not as enjoyable as Ana's last years at work. However, I was thankful that I still had a job! As someone said, "There is always, always, always something to be thankful for."

There is always, always, always something
to be thankful for.

Ana's Last Years at Work, 2005 and Beyond

As of 2005, Ana had worked as a GI (gastrointestinal) nurse at three hospitals in the Denver area. (See pictures at end of the book.) She was looking for a full-time position at any hospital. She learned of an open position at Exempla Good Samaritan Hospital. When she went for an interview, the position was already filled. However, she was told of another position in pre-op surgery. Ana called about the job and was invited to complete an application. Ana was then interviewed and hired as a full-time employee. Other GI nurses were not satisfied with their jobs and wanted to work in pre-op surgery. However, Ana had taken the last full-time pre-op position. No other full-time positions were available until Ana retired. Again, God led her to apply for that position. It was the first time that she had weekends and holidays off in her twenty-year career. We wished this could have been when our children were young.

Ana had a supervising nurse who had treated her unfairly. Ana was often assigned to patients with infectious diseases. When the work load was light, Ana would consistently be the first employee sent home rather than the part-time or nurses on call. She was an hourly employee, so this decreased her income. One day, at their regular morning meetings, the supervising nurse asked whether anybody had any concerns. Having kept the burden to herself, Ana stood and told what was happening. Everyone in the meeting was surprised at Ana's courage. Eventually, the nurse in charge apologized to Ana, and they became friends. Still, after annual reviews that gave

Ana satisfactory or improved performance ratings, she was given the smallest increases in wages. She recalled the biblical scripture, "God opposes the proud but give grace to the humble" (1 Peter 5:5 NIV).

One time, Ana filed an incident report. As usual, at pre-op surgery, the nurses prepared the patients for surgery. A patient was supposed to have a surgery on the right hip. After talking to the patient and getting the consent signed, the surgeon marked the left hip for surgery. Without hesitation, Ana grabbed the doctor's hand and said, "Sorry, Doctor, this is the wrong side!" The doctor looked at the signed consent, apologized, and corrected his error. However, the nurse-in-charge had heard the entire conversation. Afterward confirming it with Ana, the nurse suggested that Ana complete an incident report. Ana was then called before the Leadership Committee including the hospital president to tell what had happened. She was highly praised and recognized by an award. Also she received a larger increase in her paycheck.

At Ana's retirement party, her coworkers and our running group came to celebrate. One of the coworkers prepared and organized an album with pictures and notes signed by all of their department, including doctors, anesthesiologists, nurses, and office staff. The album was given to Ana at the party. One of the outstanding notes said, "Ana, your quietness is our strength." In the midst of these events, God always guides you to the right path so Ana recalls Psalm 32:8 (NIV): "I will guide you along the best pathway for your life."

Throughout Ana's long and varied career in nursing, she had many challenges, hardships, and other difficulties; but she always provided the best patient care possible. She survived and thrived through every adversity, certainly earning every dollar she received, helping our family's finances immensely. (See pictures at the end of the book.)

Running as a Way of Life for Me

Running became a very important passion of mine. I could get away from problems or concentrate on possible ways to try to solve them. While running, I could practically forget difficult circumstances, meditate, or just ask God to help carry my burdens. Also, running had fringe benefits of helping me stay physically fit and more mentally fit. It seemed to allow my thought processes to be clearer and better. It likely prevented severe high blood pressure, that was a major problem to close relatives. Running was all of the above and more to me. It personified endurance during the "hardships" of distance races. It enabled me to strengthen my body, mind, and spiritual well-being. It demanded discipline to train, the will to compete, and the enjoyment of either winning or losing. However, I regret that running took me away from important family responsibilities. I sincerely appreciate their understanding and support.

Whatever the pros and cons of running, it became interwoven into the fabric of my life—from helplessness to happiness and beyond. It helped motivate me to invest so much time and pain in therapy to walk again after the doctors said I would probably never walk after the automobile accident. This motivated me to run competitively again and actually run a marathon within three years of the broken leg. I give credit to God and my genetics via Him that my body could withstand the pounding of unknown numbers of miles of enjoyment and discomfort. Knee replacement surgery finally stopped a good thing. Running had been amazingly important to me before it became tons of good memories.

Running Lifestyle Starts, 1978

Perhaps, it is time for a flashback to when I started running seriously. Having a tough time studying and contacting people to help my family come to the United States, I looked from the dormitory window in early 1978. I saw someone running around the soccer field. I felt a nudge in my heart. I should go out there and run like that guy. I went back into my room, dressed for running, and went to the field to start jogging.

I should go out there and run like that guy.

Surprisingly, I was there for more than thirty minutes. That night, I slept very well. Afterward, I usually went jogging before dinner. Running had started in my life at the age of thirty-six. I had no idea of how "far it would take me!" I ran three to four times a week. After my family was allowed to join me in the United States, I still maintained my habit of running just not as much as when I lived alone. I was busier helping my family adjust to the new life, but my running would again increase greatly.

Moreover, at Ball State University, Ana took jogging, bowling, and badminton classes. In physical education, I took tennis, swimming, bowling, and soccer. (See picture at the end of the book.) We both enjoyed the physical parts, but the written tests on rules and regulations were as hard as other classes. For instance, I thought soccer class would be easier for me since I had played it when I was a little kid. The rule book was all in the English measurement system not the metric system which I knew. Also the mechanics of the game were totally different from what I thought I knew. Ana recalled her experience with playing badminton. She said not being coordinated with the racquet caused much difficulty getting the shuttlecock across the net. She said it was frustrating to her and her teammate.

Running Races, 1985

In 1985, my running increased drastically. I started participating in races on weekends. At age forty, I had started having annual physicals. My doctor advised me to lose weight and watch my diet. He said that one of the ways to lose weight was by exercising. My father had died at the age of about seventy and my mother at about eighty. Both had high blood pressure and strokes as did my oldest sister. With these health problems being common in my family, I needed to take proactive steps to avoid them. Therefore, running became my exercise and way of preventing high blood pressure.

As a drill sergeant, in the Portuguese army, I had run with my trainees. Some of them were disappointed when they learned that I was the leader of the platoon. Normally, I would push them harder than others. I could go faster and cover more miles than usual in the stipulated times. Even as a teenager, I had run long distances to and from the distant schools. Thus, it seemed that running was in my blood.

In 1985, I ran my first marathon, 26.2 miles, in Muncie. The country course was challenging with lots of hills. (See picture at the end of the book.) I trained with a friend, Brad, who became my running partner for several years. In my second Muncie Marathon, in 1988, I tried to qualify for the Boston Marathon. To qualify in my age division, I needed to run it in three hours and twenty minutes. On a flatter course, I could have easily qualified. I ran it in three hours and twenty-nine minutes, just nine minutes over. I was so close to qualifying for Boston, but it would be many years before I would reach it.

Muncie companies and corporations competed in the Corporate Challenge. I was assigned to run in the four hundred or eight hundred meters or the four hundreds four-by-four relays. We used the track-and-field at Muncie Central High School and later the Ball

State University Stadium. (See pictures at the end of the book.) We had some fast runners. The training and the running events enabled me to become faster. Before I started running, I had weighed 180 pounds. When I trained for long-distance races, I lost fifteen pounds. To balance my fitness, I incorporated weight training.

I ran in the Indy Mini (13.1 miles) from 1985 to 2006, except for 1993 and 1994, due to a car accident. I raced shorter races almost every other weekend. The registration fees were only $10 to $40. I usually ran at least one-half marathon and one marathon per year, plus several five-kilometer and ten-kilometer races.

Training for the Races

Normally, I trained five or six days a week, plus cross-training in the gym once or twice a week. My marathon training schedule was for six months and very intense. I included track interval training for speed and hills for strength. During the week, I ran six to seven miles daily (either in the mornings before work or in the evenings after work) and a long run (of ten to twenty miles) on Saturdays or Sundays. I ran forty to fifty miles weekly. Since Muncie didn't have many sidewalks or trails, my weekend runs were on streets and highways. I made sure that I always faced the oncoming traffic and maintained eye contact with the drivers.

Some people would ask Ana whether I had anything else to do at home. They saw me running on the roads very often. I give a lot of credit to Ana for allowing me to spend so much time running. It seems selfish to not have been more supportive of her. Now I realize I was addicted to running, and I apologize to her for being so self-centered.

My Car Accident, 1992

We had choir rehearsals at Eden Church on Wednesday evenings. We started practicing for the Christmas cantata at the end of October. As usual, after work on December 9, 1992, I went home from work and changed quickly into my running clothes. I ran four miles in twenty-seven minutes (6:45 pace per mile). That's how fast I ran in my training and races! I came back home, showered, ate, and drove toward the church. Going north on Walnut Street, I saw light sleet. The temperature dropped suddenly. A half mile after passing the airport, I noticed the road was becoming slick, so I slowed to less than thirty miles per hour. All of a sudden, I hit a sheet of ice. I tried to control the skid, but to no avail. I lost control of my Colt Vista minivan. It turned over and over. My seat belt broke, and I was thrown out of the vehicle and landed in the bushes a few yards from the car. I was unconscious.

Apparently, a Good Samaritan called an ambulance right away. Within fifteen minutes, I had emergency help. I vaguely heard people talking, "He is still breathing…" They cut piece by piece my new Ball Corporation jacket to determine the extent of my injuries. The ambulance took me to the emergency room right away. I was soon moved to the operation room. They found that I had broken the right femur and three ribs and had fractured my pelvis. The ribs and the pelvis were not treated, just left to heal. They inserted a metal rod inside the femur from my hip almost to the kneecap. They put a cast on me, and I stayed in the hospital for fourteen days. This was my first hospitalization in the United States.

Postsurgery

My hospital room was a large single one. It was full of flowers, plants, balloons, and get-well cards from my family, friends, and coworkers. I enjoyed the visits and encouragement of families and friends.

The prognosis was not good. My orthopedic doctor thought my running was over and that I would possibly never walk again. I took my hospital equipment home. I dedicated myself to months of painful therapy to prove my doctor wrong and to regain my mobility and running life.

> My orthopedic doctor thought my running was over and that I would possibly never walk again.

Taking showers was tough. Sometimes, one of my sons would help me to get into and out of the shower. We had no bathtub or shower handicap accessibility.

While still on crutches, I went back to work on a part-time basis until I felt comfortable enough to stay the whole day. My boss advised me to not worry about the work. He said that my getting well was his primary goal. Again, this demonstrated that I was in good standing at work.

I was convinced that God and I would not allow my walking and running abilities to be finished. I was motivated to work very hard not only to walk again but also to run distance races. I worked diligently to reach these goals. After six months of intensive physical therapy, I started walking little by little. After about ten months, I entered a five-kilometer race in downtown Muncie. I walked the entire course. I was the last to finish the race. People applauded as I came in. I got the last finisher award. It was nice to be back in a race. Then after one year, I started racing five kilometers, ten kilometers, and half marathons.

Our Fundraising Marathon, 1995

There was a fundraising race for the Leukemia Society. Ana and I joined the campaign. We were assigned to a seven-year-old boy named Corey who lived in Yorktown, a town close to Muncie. Each person needed to raise $3,000 and train for the Honolulu Marathon. This money would include the air transportation, the race registration fees, and the hotel accommodations. Each of us received a T-shirt designed with "team in training" on the front and a picture of Corey on the back. (See picture at the end of the book.)

Ana and I were committed to this charitable mission! I chose the intermediate level and Ana the beginners level of training. Training was a real challenge. During the week, we trained separately because of our schedules. On the weekends, we ran together. For a cross-training (lifting light weights, biking, and other exercises), we went two or three times each week to the gym at the Ball Memorial Hospital Wellness Center. We signed up for five- or ten-kilometer races every three months. We included one-half-marathon (13.1 miles) race in our training. The registration fees were inexpensive ranging from $10 to $30. We both bought new running shoes. As we were increasing our distances, we ran the hills at the Prairie Creek course on the weekends. From the Muncie YMCA and back, the course was about twenty-four miles which was our longest run before the race. Early on an October morning, I drove around the course and dropped off frozen water bottles at mile markers 6, 13, 15, 18, and 24. We had pouches on our belts with small bottles of Gatorade and energy bars. Our training was intense.

It was amazing that I could run so much just three years after my automobile accident. I had proven my doctor wrong! Not only could I walk, but I was running marathons. My oldest son worked as an X-ray technician for my orthopedic doctor who said, "Your dad is like an animal, an iron man!" Again, faith and hope for getting better physically, mentally, and spiritually was my motto and motivation. It reminds us of Romans 5:3–5 (NIV): "Not only so, but we also rejoice in our sufferings, because we know that suffering produces perseverance; perseverance, character; and character, hope. And hope does not disappoint us, because God has poured out his love into our hearts by the Holy Spirit, whom he has given us."

The Honolulu Marathon

Ana and I were able to raise $5,000. We were $1,000 short. The organizers accepted our fundraising amount, and we were in the race. In December 1995, we drove to the Indianapolis Airport to meet other team-in-training runners. We flew to San Francisco and then to Honolulu. We checked in the Waikiki Hotel on Friday afternoon. The suite was very nice with a king-size bed.

On Saturday, we went to the expo and got our running packets and checked the starting location. After lunch, we went to the Waikiki beach and relaxed in the water. The weather was decent, sunny and slightly warm, about eighty degrees. At night, we watched the weather forecast for the day of the race, Sunday. Bad news! The forecast was for temperatures in eighties with 90 percent humidity at 6:00 a.m. We had a carbo-loading dinner. (See picture at the end of the book.) We went to bed about 9:00 p.m. and woke up at 4:00 a.m. We went to the starting point before daylight.

In early morning, the weather was already steaming with the humidity. The temperature and the humidity were just as forecasted. The first coral runners started at 5:30 a.m. We were assigned the middle coral and started running at 6:00 a.m. There were lots of international runners. The officials estimated that thirty-three thousand started the race.

After wishing each other good luck, we kissed and hugged. I moved a little ahead of Ana. This was Ana's first marathon, and it was my seventh. Ana was calm but a little apprehensive. Runners were concerned about the weather conditions. Some runners that had run the same race in previous years were complaining that they had never seen such weather. There was a very beautiful sunrise showing along the Pacific Ocean. We ran along the coast with very amazing scenery. Sometimes, we saw the high waves rising in the ocean. It reminded me of the song "How Great Thou Art!" written by Carl Borberg in 1885. At the mile 13, I saw the first place runner passing by me on the opposite side going back to the finish line. "Wow!" everybody yelled and cheered him on. There were ambulances being used to assist and pick up many collapsed/overheated/exhausted runners.

How great thou art! (Carl Borberg)

Ana and I felt the humidity and the heat becoming more and more intense. We stopped at every water area to drink water/Gatorade. We ran eastward and turned somewhere after the mile-fifteen mark and headed back toward the finish line. During the run, we had Corey on our minds. Thank God we both survived and finished. It was a victory for me running three years after the car accident. It was a victory for Ana completing her first marathon under such adverse conditions. I finished in four hours and ten minutes, and Ana finished in four hours and twenty-five minutes. (Actually, she beat the future times of our two oldest sons, Anibal and Azevedo, in the Chicago Marathon).

I waited for Ana at the finish line. She was very exhausted like I was. I congratulated her; and we kissed, hugged, and rejoiced for our great victories! These were not only for us but also for Corey's well-being. We left the finish line still exhausted and groggily walked very slowly to the hotel. We were both limping side by side, holding hands. The walk seemed like another marathon! The hotel appeared miles away, but it was only about a mile. We took showers, ate, and took a long nap. We were glad we had a king-size bed. We could not touch each other while sleeping. We had excruciating pain and aching muscles all over our bodies.

The next day, newspaper reported that only about twenty-seven thousand of the thirty-three thousand runners had finished the race, because of the weather conditions. This made us more proud of being among the finishers.

On Tuesday morning, a limousine took us to the airport, where we rode in a small plane to Kawai. It was nice to see the ocean and the small islands from the air. It was very beautiful scenery. We were still recovering from the big race and could not walk fast. We toured part of the awesome island including the big falls. We flew back at the end of the day. On Wednesday, we walked around Honolulu. We found that some prices were high. We paid $8 for a pineapple at the plantation where it had been grown. So much for things cheaper on the farm.

On Thursday morning, we flew back to the States. (See picture at the end of the book.) It had been a good experience over all. Ana decided to not run any more marathons. She stuck with halves (13.1 miles) as her longest races. She has been proud of her first, last, and only marathon; and so am I. The most important thing was that it was for a great cause—running the "team in training" for Corey!

Running Races Continue

After the Honolulu marathon, we kept racing five kilometers, ten kilometers, and the Indy-Mini (13.1 miles). My goal was still to run in the Boston Marathon. I was chasing that event like a dog chasing a car. I was told that the Chicago Marathon was a good one for qualifying for the Boston Marathon. Being a flat course with lots of room for cheering fans improved the chances. I had run it twice before but had been unable to run a qualifying time.

In the beginning of 2006, Sally, one of my best running partners and a good friend of the family, invited me to train with her. We could run in the Chicago Marathon again to hopefully qualify for Boston. I said that would be impossible since I had already tried it twice, but to no avail. She insisted on the training, so finally I accepted her challenge and help. As usual, we followed the intermediate training chart. During the week, we trained separately and ran longer distances together or in a running group on the weekends. (See pictures at the end of the book.)

The Chicago Marathon, 2006

The second Sunday of October was race day. Ana, our friend Sally, and I flew from Denver on Friday. Sally went to meet someone she knew from South Africa, so we didn't see her again until race day. Arlindo and Anibal and their families drove from Indiana and stayed at other hotels.

Cicero and Azevedo had trained to run with me. Living in Chicago, Cicero made arrangements for us to spend the night close to the starting area. The apartment was high in a tall building. We could see everything outside and on the building's lower level through the large windows.

Ana and I had a queen-sized bed in the bedroom, and Azevedo had a mattress on the floor in the living room. Azevedo did not sleep well as he anxiously anticipated his first marathon. On the other hand, I slept well. I felt prepared and confident, but I was still apprehensive since I had already failed twice in Chicago to qualify for Boston.

About 4:30 a.m., Ana and I woke up and found that Azevedo was already up. We walked about a mile to the starting line. We met Cicero at the corals indicated. There were many runners with their families to cheer and support. Cicero was faster than any of us, so

185

he was placed in the front coral. I was put in the middle coral and Azevedo in the later coral.

One can move down to a lower coral (slower time) but not vice versa. So Cicero decided to start with me. We had pacer waves, which were groups of runners running at specific speeds to finish at planned times. My qualifying time for Boston was four hours. Therefore, we joined that wave and positioned ourselves in front. I found that the high-altitude training in Denver helped me run easier in the lower altitude in Chicago. Also the excitement and adrenalines caused me to feel very good. We were running at speeds of less than eight minutes per mile. At that speed, I could qualify with time to spare. We saw Ana and other members of the family at ten kilometers, then at mile 13.1 (half marathon). Cicero and I were moving so well that all of a sudden we found ourselves running with the wave 3:45 pacers, fifteen minutes faster than the four-hour qualifying time. Cicero said, "Whoa, dad! Are you okay? I think you need to slow down." After mile 14, Cicero asked me whether I was still okay before he ran ahead much faster to run his race rather than assist mine. Then gradually I had to slow my pace. At mile 18, my legs started hurting.

Go, go, go! (Ana)

Dad, let's finish together. Don't walk. Let's go. Let's go. Let's go! (Cicero)

The families had taken a train from downtown to China Town at miles 20 and 21. At mile 23, I started having cramps in my hamstrings. I stepped aside and stretched and then ran slowly. At mile 24, I saw some members of my family. It was encouraging to see them again cheering loudly! I had mantras in my mind, "I can do all things through Christ who gives me strength" (Philippians 4:13 NIV). The wave 3:45 pacers passed me. I was very discouraged and cramping badly.

At mile 24, I saw Anibal and Arlindo and their families. I had another scripture in my mind, "Since I am surrounded with the crowds of witness…let's run the race with perseverance the race marked out for us… He endured the cross" (Hebrews 12:1–2 NIV). Jesus endured the cross for our sins, and I was enduring the race trying to make the qualifying time for Boston. I felt surrounded by my family along the race and was determined to finish. At mile 25, Ana ran with me for a short time and then said, "Go, go, go!" I was hurting all over my body. Before turning up a slight hill to the finish line, Cicero showed up and ran with me. I felt that I must walk, but Cicero said, "Dad, let's finish together. Don't walk. Let's go. Let's go. Let's go!" A few yards before the finish line, he stepped off the course, and I tried to sprint to it. He came and hugged me. A *Chicago Tribune* reporter and photographer interviewed and photographed us for the next morning's paper (not pictured in the book).

I had finished in 3:59:56. Hooray, I had finished under four hours! I had accomplished my twenty-year dream of qualifying to run in the Boston Marathon. I had not seen the wave four pacers, because I had finished in front of them. It had taken almost four years to get my family to the United States. It had taken more than five times that many years to qualify for Boston and by only four seconds.

> Dreams are achieved in sleep. Goals are
> achieved through hard work. (Unknown)

My dream had come true! I was reminded of the prophetic scriptures from Joel 2:28 (NIV): "I will pour out my spirit on all people. Your sons and daughters will prophesy, your old men will dream dreams, your young men will see visions." I have heard someone say, "Dreams are achieved in sleep. Goals are achieved through hard work."

This race taught me to be faithful, perseverant, and hopeful but also to have supporters to help. An African proverb states, "If you want to go quickly, go alone. If you want to go far, go together."

> If you want to go quickly, go alone. If you
> want to go far, go together. (African proverb)

I was very thankful for my family members because they had enabled me to run a qualifying time. George Santayana, a philosopher, said, "The family is one of the masterpieces." There could be no doubt that without family support, I could not have qualified by running four seconds faster than another miss of the Boston Marathon.

The family is one of the masterpieces.
(George Santayana)

Preparation for the Boston Marathon

I could design my own training. I had already run fifteen marathons: four in Muncie, three in Indianapolis, one in Columbus, three in Chicago, one in Honolulu, and three in Denver, plus many halves (13.1 miles), nine miles, ten kilometers, and five kilometers. I planned to do the same training for Boston, but winter weather greatly restricted my outdoor running. I did utilize the Recreation Center in Thornton, Colorado. I did cross-training—took spinning classes twice a week, did body pumps once a week, lifted light weights for the whole body, and ran on the treadmill for ninety minutes per day. When the weather was suitable, I ran distances outside mainly on weekends because of my work. Our training group had three to six people. Thus, peer pressure helped us to keep our training commitments. I looked forward to good weather. By the end of February, the weather improved, so we could run outside more. I ran the hills at least twice a week. I went to the gym twice a week for conditioning.

My last long practice run was three weeks before the race followed by tapering off. I concentrated on eating well—three meals a day and sleeping at least seven hours each night. Besides my running buddies, Ana was my best motivator. We sometimes ran together the first few miles while I was warming up my legs.

The Boston Marathon, 2007

On April 13, 2007, Ana and I flew to Boston from Denver. We met our son Cicero, daughter-in-law Vera, and their two-year-old daughter, Carolina, from Chicago. Also our daughter, Clarisse; her husband, Dana; and two-year-old son, David, from the Washington, DC, metropolitan area were there. I had my cheerleaders and support ready. (See picture at the end of the book.) It was cloudy on Friday afternoon as we toured the city. We enjoyed dinner with the whole family.

On Saturday morning, rain started and continued the whole day. In the afternoon, we got my running package from the Expo. My bib number was 18,814. I bought a jacket and a sweater with the Boston Marathon logo as souvenirs. By then, the rain was pouring. The weather forecast was bad news. It would be cold and rainy all day Sunday and well into race day, Monday. I thought, *Oh well, I have made it to the elite race whatever the circumstances.* On Sunday, we relaxed mostly inside the hotel. Whenever we looked outside, we saw heavy rain.

On Monday morning, we woke up, about 5:00 a.m. I ate a bagel with peanut butter and jelly and orange juice. I dressed in a dark running suit, a green rain jacket, and a gray T-shirt with a heavy cap. We caught the bus to my wave. There were four waves loading at different times based on the starting times. My bus wave was the last, leaving at 8:55 a.m. The shuttles took all the runners to the Athletes' Village in Hopkinton. The rain was still coming down like crazy. The water was running everywhere on streets and sidewalks. They showed us where we could wait until the race. It was in a big tent where the water was running high. I was standing in a pool of water. Some runners had rubber boots; others had heavy plastics wrapping from feet to legs. It was chaos inside the tent. The horrible weather reminded me of the Honolulu weather on the day of the race. While at that marathon the weather had been hot, extremely humid, and sunny, Boston's was completely the opposite—rainy, cloudy, and cold. Of course, the weather for marathons is seldom perfect.

Commemorating 110 years in 2006, the Boston Athletic Association moved the starting time from noon to 10:00 a.m. For the 111th in 2007, they decided to start even earlier. The starting division times were the mobility impaired division (para athletes were only added to Boston Marathons) at 9:00 a.m., the wheelchair division at 9:25, the elite women at 9:35, the elite men at 10:00, and wave two at 10:30. I was in the last wave. There were 23,500 runners.

Ana and Clarisse and her family drove to see me at various mile markers. At 10:30 a.m., we started our wave. At mile 6.2, I saw Ana and Clarisse with her family. Many of the spectators were running along the course cheering for the runners. I just gave a thumb up to my family, telling them I was okay. Then I saw Cicero at mile 10. (He and his family left then to catch their flight back to Chicago). Ana, Clarisse, and the family were again at mile 13.1. From there, they drove to the finish line. The rain stopped, but it was still cold and wet. The course was packed with cheering spectators. There were slight and steep hills, especially the one close to Boston College after mile 20. I was tired and struggled to run that hill, so I walked and ran. I was feeling all my sixty-four-plus years. Again, I pulled out my scripture mantras one by one as I was running: "Surrounded by such a great cloud of witnesses...run with perseverance the race" (Hebrews 12:1 NIV). I even recalled my ancestors such as my dad, my mom, my sisters, and my friends being the cloud of witnesses watching me run. "I can do all things through Christ who strengthens me" (Philippians 4:13 NIV). "Those who hope in the Lord...they will soar on wings like eagles; they will run and not grow weary, they will walk and not be faint" (Isaiah 40:31 NIV).

Exhausted and sweaty, I finished in four hours, fifty-two minutes, and thirty-one seconds. My family members were waiting for me and took pictures. It was so ironic that the race that I had dreamed of for twenty years was the slowest of the sixteen marathons I had run. I was like the dog who caught the car he was chasing but could not do anything with it. I did not really care about the finishing time. I had finally accomplished my dream at the age of almost sixty-five years. I realized that the love and support of my family were much more important than the finishing time of any race. I was also very thankful for my good friend Sally, who had motivated me to train, run well in Chicago, and qualify to run in the Boston Marathon. (See pictures at the end of the book.)

Nearing the End of Racing Career

The key of training and running is to be heathy. For instance, in 2009, I had signed up for the Fort Collins Marathon. While I was training, my right knee became painful. This is the same leg that I had broken in the automobile accident in late 1992. The pain became worse and worse, but I kept running despite it. I took injections and tried several other remedies without success. I had to change the marathon to a half (13.1 miles). On the day of the race, I used a knee brace. After running four miles, the pain got worse. I had to run and walk. The faster walkers passed me, not a good sign. I struggled but finally finished the race. Ana and others had waited, waited, and waited! Seeing the faster walkers finishing, I saw they became apprehensive. Finally, I finished the race with the slower walkers limping and crying. That was my last running race. The unbearable pain ended my racing career at age sixty-seven, actual age.

Knee Replacement, 2010

Since I was having so much pain in my knee, I decided to seek medical help. I went to an orthopedic doctor who took an X-ray and determined that bone was scraping bone. All the cartilages had worn away. On April 1, 2010, I had total knee replacement surgery. The doctor advised me to never run again, just walk, bike, hike, or do low-impact exercises. This change was very devastating for me since running had been my passion. It was hard to adjust and accept the challenge. I prayed to God to heal me so I could run again. However, I was reminded of Paul asking God to remove a thorn from his flesh: "But He said to me (Paul): 'My grace is sufficient for you, for my power is made perfect in weakness'" (2 Corinthians 12:9 NIV). As of 2020, my knee is still well. I realize His grace is sufficient for me just to walk again! I have been participating in short-distance walking races, taking spinning classes and lifting light weights. I walk with only minor limping and discomfort. Ana and I walk around neighborhood or on trails averaging ten to fifteen miles a week. I will never be able to run again, but I feel like I did all that circumstances and my body would permit. Moreover, now I contemplate seeing all my medals, the Boston and the Chicago hats, and the running statistics hanging on the garage wall. (See pictures at the end of the book.) I am truly thankful for God allowing me to still be physically active after the amazing number of miles that I ran.

My Running More Than Forty-Eight Thousand Miles in Thirty-One Years

Before I started running, I had no idea of how much abuse my body would absorb and the enjoyment my mind would experience from my running for recreation, exercise, training, and racing. When challenged, I carefully estimated the miles I ran each month for thirty-one years. My calculated total was 48,430 miles, an average 1,562 miles per year, 130 miles per month, and 4.3 miles per day. This was equivalent to seventeen trips from New York City to San Francisco. Assuming I averaged six miles per hour, this running would have taken 8,072 hours or 336 days. My actual age during this time ranged from thirty-six to sixty-seven. Amazingly, I averaged almost two thousand miles per year (over five miles per day) while in my sixties.

The total miles ran could have been more except for many lost miles recovering from the broken leg that caused my doctor to say that I would possibly never walk again. It took about four months of therapy before I could walk without crutches. Furthermore, the early family adjustment, winter weather, and my not starting serious distance running younger likely reduced the number of miles significantly, if my body could have survived it.

Retirements and Activities

Since I was legally sixty-six (actually sixty-eight chronologically), I decided against returning to work after the knee-replacement surgery. On July 1, 2010, I officially retired from Ball Corporation. In December 2012, Ana had rotator cuff surgery, so she decided to retire as well at age sixty-six in February 2013. Having been so busy in school, rearing kids, running, and working all our lives, retirement was very different for both of us.

Before retirement, we both had tried to put God first. The biblical scriptures say, "But seek first the kingdom of God and his righteousness, and all these things will be given to you as well" (Matthew 6:33). We believed that we should start each day reading the Bible and devotionals, as well as meditating and praying together. Each morning, we needed and wanted to connect to God before doing anything else. As Jesus said in John 15:7 (NIV), "If you remain in me and my words remain in you, ask whatever you wish, and it will be given you." Also the hymn by Annie S. Hawks encourages and reminds us, "I need thee every hour."

I need thee every hour. (Annie S. Hawks)

Having different work schedules, couple devotionals seldom worked for us. Ana woke up at 4:30 a.m., and I did at 6:00 a.m. During the week, Ana and I usually had our spiritual moments separately, often quick devotionals and prayers, except on the weekends or holidays. At night, we could seldom do much either, because we were both exhausted from long days of work and Ana having to get up early for work.

After our retirements, we were very pleased that we could accomplish our priorities better. It has been like the Spanish proverb "It is a beautiful thing to do nothing and then rest." We can usually wake up whenever we wish without an alarm clock. After getting up, we take our time to prepare ourselves for spiritual moments.

> It is a beautiful thing to do nothing and then rest. (Spanish proverb)

After taking this devotional time, we feel connected to God who provides us with nourishment, support, love, and care that we need to give to others during the day. Then we plan our daily activities, such as household, errands, exercise (going to the gyms or taking a walk, etc.), and volunteering at our church or in the community. Despite the Spanish proverb, we were never "geared" for just leisure and rest.

Our Moving Back to Indiana, 2013

We moved closer to our families, another high priority. We invested much in rearing our children under challenging circumstances. We wanted to see the fruits of our labors (especially Ana's) as much as possible. We love to see our grand children's school and sports activities. We have more time to babysit, but the need for that has vanished quickly. We can drive or fly to Washington, DC, to spend a couple of weeks or more with Clarisse and her family. Other times, we drive to Chicago to see Cicero and his family. We visit our relatives in Angola every few years.

Since most of our kids and grandchildren lived in the Midwest, we moved back to Indiana in June 2013. We chose the Indianapolis area as being somewhat central to our families. We bought a single-family one-level home in Westfield, forty minutes away from Arlindo; one hour from Anibal in Muncie and Azevedo in Lafayette; four hours from Cicero in Chicago; and a ninety-minute flight from Clarisse in the Washington, DC, area. Unfortunately, in July 2019, Arlindo and his family that were closest to us moved to Atlanta, Georgia, due to a job relocation.

We found a nearby place to worship, the Noblesville First United Methodist Church. We both enjoy singing in the chancellor choir, working on several committees, having Bible Study, serving meals, and helping with rummage sales. (See pictures at the end of the book.) I volunteer to teach English as a second language to various international students at our church. Ana volunteers at the Westfield Hospital. We volunteer at the local Food Pantry (the Hamilton County Gleaners) and at Teter Organic Farm, planting, weeding, and harvesting. I also volunteer on behalf of our church in writing letters to legislators (Indiana senators, congressmen) to advocate the Bread for the World's Offering of Letters.

Our Fiftieth Wedding Anniversary Celebration, 2016

On June 25, 2016, we celebrated our fiftieth wedding anniversary at the Noblesville First United Methodist Church in Indiana. Besides our families, we invited our old and dear friends from Eden Church, in Muncie, Indiana, including Carmichaels, Browns, Thompsons, Childs, Halls, Addingtons, Painters, Hennigars, Oranders, Beverly Cassel, Becky Roland, and Sherell Bryant. Also we invited our neighbors, the Kobilics and Knights. There were friends from our current Bible Study, the Stolzs, retired pastor Warren Otter, and his wife (deceased). Other invitees were the Wells, Paulinos, and our old friends from Eritrea and Ethiopia, the Tzegais and Bizunehs. (See pictures at the end of the book.)

Pastor Otter officiated at the renewal of our vows. Ana still had her original wedding ring. Unfortunately, I had lost mine over ten years earlier while playing outdoor volleyball. During the vows, I surprised Ana with new wedding rings for both of us. Pastor Otter joked that I was the luckiest person in the world that Ana had not left me when I lost my original ring. We felt greatly honored that almost everyone who was invited managed to attend.

Our families served a large cake, finger food, and drinks. We were very thankful to have achieved another milestone. We had gone through lots of roller-coaster-like circumstances during our married years. We had built our unwavering faith in God together despite our almost four years of family separation and my losing the wedding ring.

In August, our children honored us with a seven-day Royal Caribbean Cruise to Europe. After flying to Venice, Italy, we took a tour bus to Croatia, Greece, and Turkey. On the way back from Venice, we flew to Lisbon, Portugal, where we stayed for a couple of days visiting relatives. This was our second cruise. (See pictures at the end of the book.)

Our first cruise had been a seven-day trip in June 2006 for our fortieth anniversary. We flew to London and stayed there for a couple of days before flying to Barcelona, where we boarded the ship on the Mediterranean Sea. We went to Monaco, Rome, and Pompeii, Italy, and back to Barcelona. Both cruises were fabulous; and we enjoyed the sceneries, food, relaxation, and our time together. (See pictures at the end of the book.)

In retrospect, we remember two major milestones: our religious wedding in 1966 in Cubal, Angola, and our family reunification on July 22, 1979, in the United States of America after almost four years apart. These were our highest mountain top experiences.

Conclusions

Summary of Our Lives

Ana and I have always tried to do what we believe is right. We respected our parents and accepted their values of our education, work, and faith. We were fortunate to avoid and survive the childhood diseases that killed many in Angola. We were motivated students. We developed a strong work ethic. We met, married, and started our family. Our major family goals never changed, specifically to trust and follow God, rear a strong family, and help others to the extent possible.

> Our major family goals never changed, specifically to trust and follow God, rear a strong family, and help others to the extent possible.

Our resources, available choices, and risks became like a roller-coaster ride going up and down. We welcomed five children as our heritage from the Lord. Psalm 127:3 says, "Children are a heritage from the Lord, offspring a reward from Him." Our resources and status in Angola reached a high level for a Black family under discriminatory policies. Our status and available alternatives were excellent. The possibility of a severe civil war seemed small.

To achieve even more, we decided that I should accept a scholarship for a free college education in the United States. Soon after this decision was implemented, the situation in Angola worsened drastically. The civil war put my family's lives in jeopardy. Ana, alone, had to nurture and protect our children with the Angolan civil war all around them. There seemed to be no way that my family could escape from Angola. Eventually, they were permitted to leave Angola by faking a medical appointment in Portugal. With most of our material things lost and money spent, their lives as refugees were very difficult. With no passports, they were stranded in Portugal illegally and could not go anywhere else. Enduring hardships was an everyday necessity for my family and me.

Although I was safe in the United States, I did not know whether my family was alive for eight months. If I had stayed in Angola, I would have likely been killed or imprisoned as the treasurer of UNITA, which was violently defeated. I could not return but did everything possible to reunite our family. Ironically, the loophole of me being a refugee without a country finally enabled my family to join me after being separated almost four years.

We credit God and His people for helping us survive and eventually reunite in the United States. This, too, was uncharted territory for all of us to learn a new language, adjust to a new culture, learn, work, and thrive. God and His people continued helping us in many ways until we could finally become independent so that we could help others more. Our book title truly describes much of our lives.

Our children survived their early childhood years of war, poverty, and virtual homelessness due to a strong mother and help from God and His people. They adjusted very quickly in the United States where they excelled in academics, sports, and their professions. We think they have brought honor to us, our parents, and their other African ancestors. We greatly enjoy our grandchildren's continuing successes. We hope that our lives and faith have been tributes to all who helped us. Our faith and works enabled us to reach independence (except from God) and to truly appreciate it. We believe that we earned our retirements and want to enjoy them as long as possible. Still, we look forward to the promise of eternal life with God. To God be the glory!

As mentioned previously, I am not writing this book for money. In fact, if we are fortunate enough to have our story published, any profits will be put into charitable Christian efforts for Angolan children. If readers are inspired and moved by God or their inner self to donate, we guarantee that every penny will be used to assist young Angolans in meeting their desperate educational needs. Like our parents did for us, we would "like to teach youths to fish rather than give them fish." We believe that education provides them with the tools and skills to "fish" and help others.

We frequently learn of Angolan children whose resources and alternatives are very limited. We have been able to personally help several reach their educational goals. Some of these are now doing the same for others. Sometimes just realizing that others care is the catalyst to enable people in need to succeed.

Until now we had never seriously considered forming a foundation for Angolan education or a similarly named one. We would form one if sufficient funds would cause it to be needed. Yes, faith and hard work would continue pushing us into this new uncharted territory. This seems too huge to attain. But from the biblical perspective, Jesus told His disciples, "With man this is impossible, but with God all things are possible" (Matthew 19:28 NIV). Just as God and His people helped us so much, we wish we had more resources to provide assistance to others who have massive needs.

Who I Am and Who I Am Not

As we near completion of our book, I think it is appropriate that I provide my perception of some things about who I am and who I am not. I am the product of a challenging childhood, hardworking and loving parents, and motivation for as much schooling as feasible. I was recruited into the Portuguese army and was a drill sergeant. I graduated from Ball State University with a BS in natural resources and biology and with an MA in computer science. I worked at Ball Corporation in Muncie, Indiana, and then in Denver, Colorado, as a computer programmer for twenty years and as a mail room specialist for six years.

I am a husband of more than fifty years, a father of five children, grandfather of fifteen grandchildren, and one great-grandchild, so far. I prioritize my time by putting God first, my family second, and then others. I am a devoted Christian who goes to church regularly, who wakes up every morning and reads together with my wife the *Upper Room* devotional book and other devotionals along with related scriptures in the Bible and pray. I trust in God's provision and believe in the power of prayer.

I love music and taught myself how to read the music from the piano keyboard. I built a guitar and played it while in Angola. I sing in choirs and participate on church committees.

I devote much leadership to the CROP Walk (fighting world hunger). I volunteered at the Community, Faith, Hope and Love in Indianapolis. I volunteer helping teach English as a second language in our church. (See pictures at the end of the book.) I am involved in the church Bible studies, gardening, and as a church liturgist.

I am a perfectionist, patient, positive, perseverant, resilient, pragmatic, detail-oriented, and known as a hard worker. When I make a commitment, I intend to keep it. If I mean no or maybe, then I do not commit.

I am a positive thinker. The former prime minister of the United Kingdom Winston Churchill said, "The positive thinker sees the invisible, feels the intangible, and achieves the impossible."

> The positive thinker sees the invisible, feels the intangible, and achieves the impossible. (Winston Churchill)

I was competitive in running distance races. The wear and tear that my body absorbed and my mind enjoyed for the amazing number of miles I ran is almost unbelievable.

I was recognized with an integrity award in Delaware County, Indiana.

I believe in family unity and preventive care.

I cry with someone who cries and laugh with someone who laughs.

I am a certified volleyball official for high and middle schools.

Finally, I am actually two years older than my official birth certificate age, and on some days, I feel it.

I am not a biblical scholar, a psychologist, an evangelist, or an artist/designer, a medical doctor, or a ballplayer.

Ana, Who I Am and Who I Am Not

I am a proud wife and mother of five lovely children. I have fifteen grandchildren and one great-grandchild, so far.

I am a graduate of Indiana Wesleyan University and passed the STATE BOARD exam to become a registered nurse.

I worked at various hospitals in different departments for twenty-five years with the last seven years in pre-op surgery in Denver being the most enjoyable.

I prioritize my time by putting God first, family second, and then others. I am a devoted Christian.

I sing in choirs and participate in women's activities, food pantry, and dinners-on-us.

I help lead the CROP Hunger Walk and volunteer at Westfield Hospital. I volunteered at the Community, Faith, Hope and Love in Indianapolis. (See pictures at the end of the book.) I help women at the Riverview Hospital crochet. I participated in the Emmaus Women Walk in 2016.

I follow my instincts in making decisions and am very observant.

I am known as a quiet person who is strong inside. For much of my life, the Bob Marley's song lyrics applied: "You never know how strong you are until being strong is the only choice you have."

> You never know how strong you are until being strong is the only choice you have. (Bob Marley)

I don't hold grudges, and I smile to all I encounter, keeping my mind positive.

I love to help. I can give and receive. I am kind and caring, crying with someone who cries and laughing with someone who laughs.

I am a good copilot when we travel.

I am not a public speaker, schoolteacher, artist, or ballplayer.

Which God Are We Serving?

We serve the God of whom Joshua said, "But if serving the Lord seems undesirable to you, then choose for yourselves this day who you will serve, whether the gods your forefathers served beyond the River or the gods of the Amorites, in whose land you are living. But as for me and my household, we will serve the Lord" (Joshua 24:15 NIV).

We serve the unseen God of whom Jesus said to Thomas, "Have you believed because you have seen me? Blessed are those who have not seen and yet come to believe" (John 20:29 NIV).

We serve the God who is always with us, Emmanuel, who appeared to Elijah and whispered in "a still small voice."

> Then a great and powerful wind tore the mountains apart and shattered the rocks before the Lord, but the Lord was not in the wind. After the wind there was an earthquake, but the Lord was not in the earthquake. After the earthquake, came a fire, but the Lord was not in the fire. And after the fire, came a gentle whisper. When Elijah heard it, he pulled his cloak over his face and went out and stood at the mouth of the cave. Then a voice said to him, "What are you doing here, Elijah?" (1 Kings 19:11–13 NIV)

With this God present, we were able to maintain our faith during difficult times. And our continuing faith in the unseen Lord can serve as a powerful witness to others.

Final Thoughts

Our conclusion is that like with everyone else, God never gave up on us. He saw our potential and remembered why He made us. We were created for great things. We trusted in Him with our hearts and souls at the time of adversities, and we gave thanks to Him for what He has done for us. As we live longer, we discover that we can no longer physically do the things we did when we were younger. However, we have become more experienced and mature, hopefully with increased wisdom with the right attitude to the world around us.

The biblical scriptures give us promises of God by saying, "Even to your old age and gray hairs, I am He, I am He who will sustain you. I have made you and I will carry you; I will sustain you and I will rescue you." Also the Apostle Paul writes, "Though outwardly we are wasting away, yet inwardly we are being renewed day by day" (2 Corinthians 4:16 NIV).

I survived diseases and a major car accident. Ana, with five little kids, endured the Angolan civil war and poverty in Portugal. Despite our many challenges, our children are all educated, independent, and well employed, and have their own families. So we continue to trust Him and try to help those in need to the extent that we can.

The American motto is 'In God we trust." We trust God because God is in control of everything. In the Bible, the disciples were amazed when Jesus calmed the storms: "What kind of man is this? Even the winds and the waves obey him" (Matthew 8:27 NIV)!

Like in the following hymn, God sent God's only Son in human form to live among us. Jesus suffered like us but much worse. He was crucified on the cross to bear our sins. He died, but on the third day, He rose from the dead. Victory!

Our lives, struggles, and love for others remind us of Christ Jesus. This is a Savior we serve. "He lives. He lives. Christ Jesus lives today!" He lives among us! He lives within our hearts by *faith*!

This is from my favorite hymn "He Lives" by Alfred H. Ackley, 1933:

> I serve a risen Savior, He's in the world today;
> I know that He is living, whatever men may say;
> I see His hand of mercy, I hear His voice of cheer,
> And just the time I need Him He's always near.
> He lives! He lives! Christ Jesus lives today!
> He walks with me and talks with me along life's
> narrow's way.

He lives! He lives! Salvation to impart!
You ask me how I know he lives? He lives within
my heart!

This is Ana's prayer:

O Lord, may the hope you give us be so evident
that others will want to read these words of
our story. Help us to be ready for opportunities to
witness to your love and salvation, amen!

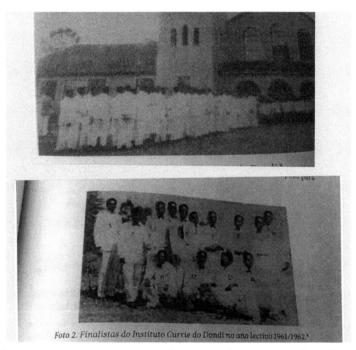

Foto 2. Finalistas do Instituto Currie do Dondi no ano lectivo 1961/1962.

(Above) Currie Institute in Dondi Mission high school class of 1962
with about two hundred seniors; (bottom) group from Lutamo
Mission in Dondi; (back row) Joe Chimbanda (third from the
left) and Gerviz Satima (fifth from the left)—two of the known
survivors (all died either of the civil war or natural disease).

Achievements and Graduation

Award by Dr. Don Van Meter at Natural Resources Department, 1979

Pregraduation party with all faculty members

Ladd and Vyas (master's degree), August 1984

Ball State University, BS degree, May 1980
Friends from Malawi and Namibia, Africa

Family
Congrats, Joe/Dad!

With friends from Zimbabwe and Mali, Africa

Pin ceremony at Indiana Wesleyan University, May 1991

I made it!
Thanks God!

Norma congratulates Ana on her graduation.

At our first home we owned in Muncie, 1991.

Joe giving thanks for being honored with the
Integrity Enhancement Award 1996

Farewell party moving to Denver, Colorado;
Joe relocated with Ball Corporation, 1998;
Family and friends

Visiting with friends from Eritrea and Ethiopia (the Tzeggais and Bizunehs) in Indianapolis during our trip back from Denver, 2011.

Outreach Mission

Joe playing a pump organ

Igreja (church) Peregrinos Huambo playing pump organ, 1973

Directing choir and playing the pump organ, 1973

Ontario, Canada,
former Angolan missionaries at Angolan Memorial Scholarship meeting

Mississauga loading clothes shipped to Angola
Dr. Allen Knight, July 1977

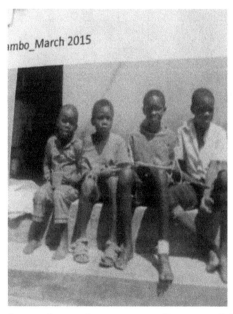

Four Angolan orphans whose parents disappeared during the
war. Joe and Ana arranged placement at an orphanage, 2014

After two years (2017), they are happy with the new
"mother" at the orphanage. They are part of the
inspiration for the Chimbanda Scholarship Fund.

Clarisse Samukuenda, student in law school in Angola and
sponsored by NFUMC; Huambo, Angola, 2014

A church built in Xangongo, Angola, by Darrell Hockersmith;
son Paul, an architect; and Bob Vasques, and me, 2005

Rev. Jerry Rairdon NFUMC
(Noblesville First United Methodist Church) Hamilton
County CROP Hunger Walk, 2016

Carolyn Reed walked with us to fight the
hunger locally and globally, 2017

Clarisse Sacato visiting from Lubango, Angola, 2019

NFUMC volunteering at Teter Organic Farm, 2019. Ana is weeding.

Hope, Faith,
Love, 2018; Ana is ready to help and pray with a client.

Group leaders in Hope, Faith, Love, 2018

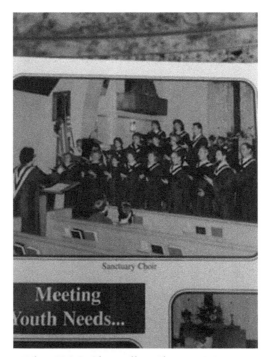

Eden UCC Chancellor Choir in Muncie,
1976–1998; Joe is in the back row.

Good Shepherd UMC Chancellor
Choir, in Thornton, Colorado, 1999–2013.
Joe is singing a Christmas solo.
Ana is in the back row singing alto led by Stacy Lang.

Noblesville First UMC Christmas performance; Chancellor Choir led by
Dr. Jeff Wright, 2013–2020.
Joe is in the back row, third from the right.

Ana is in the second row, second from the right.

English as a Second Language Program teachers and volunteers at NFUMC, 2019; Joe is in the back row.

Cruises

For our fortieth anniversary,
our children helped buy tickets for our trips to
Barcelona, Monaco, Rome, and Pompeii.

In Rome in 2006, we saw Pope Benedict XVI
parading at the cathedral.

Fiftieth anniversary, 2016 (Venice, Croatia, Greece, Turkey), at Croatia.

Walking out of the ship and heading to a town in Turkey to buy souvenirs.

Our family and relatives celebrating our golden anniversary at Noblesville First UMC, Indiana, in 2016. We exchanged vows, and it was officiated by our retired pastor, Warren Otter.

Career and Hobbies

IT Glass Department at Ball Corporation in Muncie, 1988

Ball IT Department in Muncie Christmas party, 1984–1996

P. Stanely, manager, giving me a gift for a Quarter
Century Ball Corporation, 2009.

Ana standing in front of our Ball State Family Housing. Coming from
work at the nursing home while going to nursing school!
May 1980

Pinning ceremony at
the Indiana Wesleyan University, May 199.

At North Sububan Hospital GI Lab with Sue the
bottom picture shows the lab, 2009.

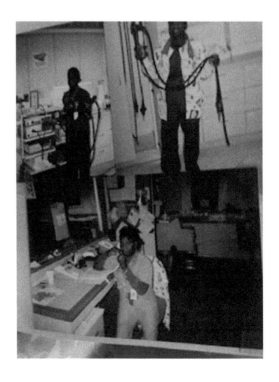

Emiko, one of her buddies at Exampla Hospital, Denver Colorado, 2011.

Ready for retirement from Exampla Hospital,
Denver, Colorado,
2012. Bye!

Dr. Kinnary at the surgical unit at Exampla Hospital.
She was very generous supporter of charities!

Jo Munsel, Ana's coworker, made up an album with all the staff
signatures to cherish our friendship and comradeship.

While awaiting family to come playing tennis;
at Ball State University, 1978.

Corporate challenge four-by-four relay at Ball Corporation, 1998.

After 4x4 relay at Ball Corporation, 1998.

Training for Muncie Marathon – 1985

Training for my first marathon with Brad Muncie in 1985.

Preparing for Honolulu Marathon;
team in training for Cory (leukemia) in Muncie in 1995.

Carbo loading in Waikiki Hotel, Honolulu in 1985.

Welcome back home in Muncie from Honolulu, 1995.

Ana with Sally – 13.1 Miles

Ana and Sally in Denver, Colorado, 2000.

Boulder Bolder
2001

Celebrating Anibal and Lydia's short-lived miracle twin girls by running
Indy Mini Marathon (13.1 miles); seven Chimbandas in 2002.

After Boulder Bolder 10K race, 2003.

Memories from Chicago Marathon in 2006.

Vera, Carolina (two), David (two), Grandma Ana, and
Clarisse cheerleading at Boston Marathon.

Starting at the Boston Marathon in the bottom
photo and finishing in the top photo, 2007.

Results

Boston Marathon statistics in 2007.

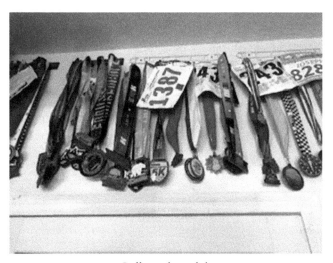

Collected medals

Epilogue

What if circumstances had been different for Ana and me?

Anyone can wonder how things would have happened differently if many past incidents had not occurred exactly as they did. Ana and I believe that God and God's people protected, nurtured, and assisted us due to His plans for us and our faith, efforts, and persistent prayers. Thus, we believe that divine help rather than random chance determined our major experiences. Still, it is interesting to ponder what-ifs.

> What if circumstances had been different for Ana and me?
> Anyone can wonder how things would have happened differently if many past incidents had not occurred exactly as they did.

What if I had not survived the two-year battle with smallpox in childhood? (This was during an era of poor medical care and many childhood fatalities in Angola. Three of my six siblings died before reaching six years of age despite our parents' strong efforts and prayers.) I was unconscious for three months, unable to pray, and with a yet-to-be developed faith. However, my parents' faith was strong, and I certainly believe that they prayed diligently for my recovery while working amazingly hard providing full-body applications of a soothing mixture every day for four months. If I had not survived smallpox or Lyme disease or extremely severe diarrhea, none of our descendants would exist.

Several specific circumstances resulted in Ana and me meeting, falling in love and getting married. Any little change could have prevented these life highlights. My diligence as a student and shyness prevented me from having other potential-wife girlfriends before Ana. Various situations enabled Ana to become a well-known radio broadcaster, be brought her to my attention, and boost my confidence to approach her. It helped to be able to mention that our good friends knew one another. If Ana had not expressed a need for a math tutor, it is very likely that we would not have become acquainted well enough to date, fall in love, and get married—all things necessary for our descendants to become realities.

Five children later and living comfortably, Ana and I decided that I should accept a full-ride scholarship for college in the United States. We anguished over the decision and prayed long and hard for guidance. We agreed for me to go and leave her to manage the household and our young children. Thus, I vacated my job as treasurer of UNITA. What happened? The government collapsed, and civil war endangered Ana and our children and depleted our material possessions. The family was unable to join me in the United States for almost four years of agony, danger, poverty, and uncertainty while any of them could have perished. Still, all survived and later thrived in the United States. Many things could have prevented these favorable outcomes. I could have lived the rest of my life regretting having abandoned my family in the attempt to improve our lives.

What if we had decided for me to stay in Angola rather than coming to the United States for college? I would likely have been imprisoned or worse, because I had been a treasurer of UNITA, which was violently defeated in the civil war.

If we had decided for me to stay in Angola, I probably would have been imprisoned or even killed since UNITA lost the civil war. My children could have never received any further financial, moral, and spiritual support from me. My grandchildren and other descendants would not have known me. Worse still, I would not have had the immense benefits of seeing them develop, mature, and succeed.

Pastor Fred Dare was the person who worked hardest (besides Ana and me) to get our family to the United States. If my three-month pastor in Illinois had not met Fred in a chance meeting, he could not have asked Fred to meet me at the airport and begin his awesome work for my family. Without many interwoven factors, we would not have benefitted from the technical, financial, and spiritual tenacity of Fred.

Ball State University was selected for me by others only because of my majoring in natural resources. If I had chosen a different major, I would probably never have come to Ball State or Muncie, where my family and I had so many life-changing events. Elsewhere, my family would have gone to other schools, got different jobs, found other spouses, and lived elsewhere. Also, my passion for running and gardening started in Muncie.

Without Norma Carmichael causing a life-changing newspaper story in Muncie, Ball Corporation leaders would not have contacted me to work for Ball Corporation in Muncie. Also, this occurred only because our sons played soccer with the Ball Corp leaders' children. I would have eventually found employment, but its location and quality can never be known. Again, a different job and location would have many unknown consequences to our entire family and the many people we have encountered.

Employment at Ball Corp enabled our children to finish high school in Muncie to fully enjoy their academics, sports, classmates, etc. My transfer to Colorado provided us with new friends and church opportunities while taking us away from many friends and church opportunities.

My automobile accident was life-threatening. My family could have lost its main breadwinner, husband, father, and grandfather and beyond. The impacts on my family (and me) would have been major.

Many people tell Ana and me that they have been blessed by knowing us. Those blessings and ours would not have occurred if circumstances had been different.

Ana and I are very honored by the kind words in this book by people we truly respect. Besides those, our former Sunday school teacher and close friend, Norma Carmichael, wrote, "What a blessing it has been to have Joe and Ana in my life. Their faith is beyond comparison." Our friend and editor, Harold Brown, wrote, "I know of no one more faithful, considerate, and kind than Joseph and Ana Chimbanda." Our former pastor, Fred Dare, wrote, "The story of the Chimbanda family is one of inspiration and an example of the true meaning of being faithful followers of Jesus Christ. To borrow from Paul, 'They have fought the good fight and run the good race.'"

What a blessing it has been to have Joe and Ana in my life. Their faith is beyond comparison. (Norma Carmichael)

I know of no one more faithful, considerate, and kind than Joseph and Ana Chimbanda. (Harold Brown)

The story of the Chimbanda family is one of inspiration and an example of the true meaning of being faithful followers of Jesus Christ. To borrow from Paul, "They have fought the good fight and run the good race." (Rev. Fred Dare)

We pray that we can live up to these much-appreciated testimonials.

Our faith, hard work, and God's plan for us enabled us to survive, endure, and thrive in uncharted territories.

Now in 2020 with the benefit of 20/20 hindsight, it is 100 percent certain that things did happen exactly as they have in our lives to date. Many of our descendants and other people are glad they did. Back when we got married, the odds of everything unfolding exactly as they did would have been miniscule. Only God could have known. Our faith, hard work, and God's plan for us enabled us to survive, endure, and thrive in uncharted territories. We think God charted our territories. We have been truly blessed.

Acknowledgments

To misuse the familiar African proverb "It takes a village to raise a child," I believe "it takes a village to live a life and write a book." We cannot adequately express our appreciation of everyone who provided innumerable acts of kindness to us in Angola, Portugal, and the United States. We hope our book can express our sincere gratitude and be a tribute to them.

Writing this book has taken more than twenty years. I wrote it little by little whenever I had time and motivation. I could not have done this without the staunchest support of my wife, best friend, soul mate, and strength of more than fifty years, Ana Isabel. She reminded me to keep writing when my motivation faltered. She wrote some of the most important parts of the book sharing her sincere memories. Our precious children encouraged us with their ideas and advice. Our son Cicero prepared a possible outline for arranging ideas and starting a framework for writing. He tirelessly encouraged me and then used his computer skills to assist with many essential organizational details. He gave me a book entitled *The Call of the Writer's Craft* by Tom Bird. Our son Arlindo and his wife, Katie, made numerous editorial improvements. Other family members assisted in various ways.

We are incredibly thankful to Pastor Fred Dare, who was the key leader before, during, and after our family reunification. His congregation at the Muncie Community UCC supported us in many awesome ways. Also, we greatly appreciated the acceptance and kindness we received at the Good Shepherd United Methodist Church in Thornton, Colorado. Their vigor in accepting and expanding the CROP Walk was heartwarming. Our special friend there, Karen Bueno, made many improvements in our manuscript.

The Eden UCC (now Eden Church) was extremely supportive in many ways. Pastor Don Orander (deceased) helped greatly in our family's early adjustment in the United States. In addition, we feel we must acknowledge the support of the Carmichaels, Browns, Painters, Whitemans, Hennigars, Addingtons, Childs, Thompsons, and others (we cannot list them all) who heard parts of our experiences, encouraged us to write this book, and demonstrated tremendous Christian love and fellowship. In particular, we want to mention Norma Carmichael for her tremendous impact on us.

We are deeply thankful to Harold Brown, who often encouraged us and later agreed to edit the manuscript. He has been a friend of our family for more than forty years and has developed an insight into our lives. He helped to remove the "fat" from my writing without sacrificing the "meat." Together, we invested much time and effort, making drastic improvements. Also, he wrote the foreword. A special tribute is owed to Harold's wife, Lorene, who was patient with his many hours editing. She also meticulously proofread the final manuscript. Also we appreciate the Brown family, especially Kelli on grammar and Jeff on final organization.

We are sincerely grateful for all the missionaries who worked in Angola to improve lives with their love and compassion. Darrell and Barbara Hockersmith were especially helpful to us and to many other Angolans. Their son Paul is continuing their supreme efforts impacting many lives in Angola.

> He constantly reassures us that our best days
> and yours are still ahead.

Most importantly, we want to acknowledge the Lord Jesus Christ for directing our paths in every way. Only through Jesus Christ could our faith and works have enabled us to survive and thrive in uncharted territories. He constantly reassures us that our best days and yours are still ahead.

Family Is Reunited

The Jose Chimbanda family, separated by the overthrow of the Angolan government in Africa, has been reunited in Muncie. Chimbanda was already in the U.S. at the time of the coup and could not return to his home. The family includes, left to right, front row, Anibal,12, Arlindo, 7, Cicero, 9, Azevedo, 10. Back, Ana Isabel, Clarisse, 5 and Jose.

Muncie, Indiana, December 30, 1979

About the Author

Joseph and Ana Chimbanda were born to poor hardworking, loving Christian parents in beautiful Angola, Africa, in the 1940s. Despite major health risks and challenges, they survived, learned, fell in love, married, and worked hard building their life together. Soon after they had achieved comfortable living conditions, Joseph left for college in the United States. Very soon, Ana and their five children faced terrible danger due to the collapse of the government, resulting in civil war. Their safe and peaceful lives and material possessions were quickly gone. Ana, alone, had to protect and nurture their children under very risky circumstances for almost four years of fear, frustration, worry, and prayers. Hard work and help from God and friends eventually enabled them to reunite in the United States. Currently in 2020, they feel they have been blessed in innumerable ways to the extent that they can try to help others. *Their book is full of stories that describe how God performs miracles today.*

CPSIA information can be obtained
at www.ICGtesting.com
Printed in the USA
JSHW051120080522
25591JS00003B/4

9 781638 440178